Edward Augustus Freeman

History of Europe

Edward Augustus Freeman

History of Europe

ISBN/EAN: 9783337821203

Printed in Europe, USA, Canada, Australia, Japan

Cover: Foto ©ninafisch / pixelio.de

More available books at www.hansebooks.com

EDWA... ...EMAN,
TRINITY COLL...
...THE GREEK OR...

SECOND EDITION, WITH

Toronto:
JAMES CAMPBELL &
1877.

[*The Right of Translation and Reproduction is Reserved.*]

Entered according to the Act of the Parliament of Canada, in the year one thousand eight hundred and seventy-seven, by JAMES CAMPBELL & SON, in the Office of the Minister of Agriculture.

DUDLEY & BURNS,
    Printers,
        TORONTO.

CONTENTS.

CHAP.		PAGE
I.	EUROPE AND ITS INHABITANTS	5
II.	THE GREEKS	12
III.	THE GROWTH OF ROME	27
IV.	THE DECLINE OF ROME	45
V.	THE ROMAN EMPIRE IN THE EAST	54
VI.	THE FOUNDATION OF THE EUROPEAN NATIONS	64
VII.	THE AGE OF THE CRUSADES	73
VIII.	THE DECLINE OF THE TWO EMPIRES	85
IX.	THE REFORMATION AND THE RELIGIOUS WARS	95
X.	THE GREATNESS OF FRANCE.	111
XI.	THE ALLIANCE OF THE BOURBON KINGDOMS.	118
XII.	THE FRENCH REVOLUTION	128
XIII.	THE REUNION OF GERMANY AND ITALY	139

LIST OF MAPS.

		PAGE
1.	THE GREEK COLONIES	16
2.	THE ROMAN EMPIRE AT ITS GREATEST EXTENT.	43
3.	THE EMPIRE UNDER JUSTINIAN	56
4.	THE EMPIRE UNDER CHARLES THE GREAT	61
5.	EUROPE IN THE TWELFTH CENTURY	78
6.	EUROPE UNDER CHARLES THE FIFTH.	98

HISTORICAL PRIMERS.

EUROPE.

CHAPTER I.

EUROPE AND ITS INHABITANTS.

1. **The Races of Man.**—As far back as we can learn anything, we find different nations speaking different languages; that is, different nations have used different words as the names of the same things. But even when several nations speak languages which are now so unlike that they cannot understand one another, it is often easy to see that there was a time when they all spoke the same language. Thus we can see that the chief words and forms of words in several languages were once the same. When we see that what we call **night** is in German **nacht**, in Latin **noct**, and in Greek **nykt**, and when we see the same kind of likeness in a great many other words, we need not doubt that all these tongues were once only one tongue. By thus comparing many languages together, we can class the chief nations of the world under several great groups. Each of these groups now contains several nations speaking several languages, which were once one nation speaking one language. In this book it will be enough to speak of those

nations only which have at any time lived in Europe, and in those parts of Asia and Africa whose history has been always mixed up with that of Europe. These we may class under three great heads, the **Aryan** and the **Semitic** nations, and those which, whether they are all akin to each other or not, we may put together as not belonging to either of the other two classes.

2. **The Aryan Nations.**—The group of nations to which most of the nations of Europe have belonged ever since the beginning of trustworthy history is commonly called the **Aryan** group. Nearly all the languages which are now spoken in Europe and in other lands where Europeans have settled, as well as the languages which are spoken in a great part of Asia, were all once one language. The people who spoke this old Aryan language once lived all together in the middle parts of Asia, and they found out some of the most needful arts, and had got some notions of religion and government, before they began to spread in different directions. We know this, because many of the chief words which have to do with these matters are still the same in all or most of the Aryan tongues. But, long before written history begins, these old forefathers of ours began to leave their old seats and to move, some to the west and some to the south-east. Those who pushed to the south-east settled in **Persia** and northern **India**. The old language of northern India, the **Sanscrit**, has changed less than any other tongue from the first form of the common Aryan speech. The other Aryan nations pressed westward, and settled in Europe, and in the parts of Asia nearest to Europe. And from Europe men have in later times gone forth and made settlements or **colonies** in **America** and **Australia**, where they still keep the languages of those parts of Europe from which they first set out.

3. **The Semitic Nations.**—The other chief group which concerns us is that of the **Semitic**

nations, who chiefly settled in those parts of Asia which lie between the eastern and western divisions of the Aryan group. These are the **Jews, Phœnicians, Syrians,** and **Arabs.** The languages of all these nations are very nearly akin. These Semitic nations have filled a much smaller part of the world than the Aryans; but their place in history has been very great. For the three religions which have taught men to worship one God, the Jewish, the Christian, and the Mahometan, all arose among them. The Phœnicians and Arabs also have at different times made conquests and planted colonies in a large part of Africa and even of Europe.

4. **The non-Aryan Nations of Europe.**—When the Aryans first came into Europe, they found men living there who were neither Aryan nor Semitic, and whom, as they pushed on step by step, they destroyed or drove into corners. In some few parts of Europe there still are some remains of these old **non-Aryan** races. In the mountainous lands on the borders of **Spain** and **Gaul** men still speak the **Basque** tongue, which is one of the tongues which were spoken before the Aryans came. These Basques once filled all Spain, and much of western Europe, but now they are driven up into a corner. And, in another corner in the north, the **Fins** and **Laps,** the remains of another non-Aryan people, also speak a non-Aryan tongue. And in some parts of eastern Europe non-Aryan nations have come in as conquerors of Aryan nations. These are the **Hungarians** and the **Turks,** both of whom made their way into Europe in times of which the history is well known. But the Hungarians, though they have kept their non-Aryan language, have taken to the religion and manners of Europe. This the Turks have not done. Except these small remains of the nations which lived in Europe before the Aryans came, and these two non-Aryan nations who have come into

Europe in later times, all the nations of Europe, and all the European settlements in other parts of the world, speak languages which have sprung from the original Aryan stock.

5. **The Geography of Europe.**—The continent of Europe, into which the western branch of the Aryans came, is made up of a solid mass of land in the middle, which joins on to Asia without any break, and of two systems of islands, peninsulas, and inland seas to the north and south. The whole southern part of Europe is washed by the **Mediterranean Sea**, the great inland sea which lies between the three continents of Europe, Asia, and Africa. This southern part is chiefly made up of three great peninsulas, those of **Greece**, **Italy**, and **Spain**, which are cut off by mountains—the Pyrenees, Alps, and others—from the great mass of central Europe. In the Mediterranean Sea are several great islands, as **Sardinia, Sicily, Crete,** and **Cyprus,** and many smaller ones, especially in the sea which lies between Greece and Asia, called the **Ægæan Sea** or **Archipelago**. All this end of Europe is made up of islands and peninsulas, with gulfs and straits of the sea running among them. To the north again we get something of the same kind on a smaller scale. The **Baltic Sea** and its gulfs answer to the Mediterranean, and the peninsulas and islands of **Scandinavia**, that is, **Denmark, Norway, and Sweden**, keep a faint likeness to the islands and peninsulas of the south. And to the north-west of Europe lies a great group of islands, our own island of **Britain**, the other great island of **Ireland**, with many smaller ones. And **Iceland**, another great island, lies far far away to the north-west, cut off from the rest of the world.

6. **Settlement of the Aryans in Europe.**— Such were the lands into which the western branch of the Aryans began to press long before trustworthy

history begins. The two great peninsulas of Greece and Italy were settled by one branch of the Aryan family, which seems also to have spread itself over the lands near to Greece, both in Europe and in Asia. In central Europe the **Celts** came first; they pressed to the west, and settled in Gaul, the British Islands, northern Italy, and a great part of Spain. They were followed by the **Teutonic** branch, that to which we ourselves belong. These pushed upon the Celts from the east, and occupied Germany and Scandinavia, and, at a later time, the most part of Britain. The Celtic languages are now spoken only in some small parts of Gaul and the British Islands; but in Germany, Scandinavia, and the greater part of Britain, Teutonic languages are still spoken. Of these four, Greeks, Italians, Celts, and Teutons, came most of the chief nations of Europe. But beyond the Teutons came another swarm. One branch, the smallest of all, was the people of **Lithuania** and **Old Prussia**. Their tongue is now spoken by very few people, but it has changed less from the oldest Aryan tongue than that of any other people in Europe. The other branch is that of the **Slaves**, whose name in their own tongue means **glorious**, though in other tongues it has another meaning, because bondmen of Slavonic race were once very common. These are the people of Poland, Russia, and of eastern Europe, including many of the nations which are now subject to the Turks. Thus various Aryan nations, from the old Greeks onwards, have spread themselves over all Europe, save only where a few of the older people are still left, or where non-Aryan people have come in in much later times.

7. **The Three Chief Races of Europe.**—Now of all the branches of the Aryan family which have settled in Europe, three have been, at different times and in different ways, the leaders of all the rest. The first were the old Greeks; then the people

of Italy, or more truly the one Italian city of Rome; and lastly the Teutonic nations. For it was in the lands round the Mediterranean Sea that the true civilization of the world began, and it was in Greece that it began first of all. Here history, truly so called, begins, the history of men as members of a free commonwealth. The language and art of the Greeks, the works of their writers, and their buildings, have had a power over men's minds ever since. In this way, and not by conquest, Greece has influenced the world. Rome, on the other hand, influenced the world both by conquest and by giving her laws to the nations which she conquered. Under Rome all the then civilized world, all the lands round the Mediterranean Sea, in Europe, Asia, and Africa, became one empire governed by one law; and the power of that empire and of that law has never died away. For the next race which rose to the head, our own Teutonic race, did in a manner continue Rome's power, as the Teutons became half conquerors of Rome and half disciples.

8. Rome the Centre of European History.

Now of all European history Rome is the centre. The history of Europe is almost wholly made up, first, of the steps by which the older states came under the power of Rome, and secondly, of the way in which the modern states of Europe were formed by the breaking up of that power. Greece alone has a real history of its own, earlier than that of Rome and independent of it. Then in after times the chief place passed to the Teutonic nations who settled and conquered within the Roman empire, but who learned their arts, laws, manners, religion, and language from those whom they conquered. Since then the Teutonic nations have kept at the head, for, though nations speaking other languages have often done great things, yet they have done so chiefly by help of Teutonic laws and rulers. The Celts by themselves have done but little; they came too soon to hold a chief place. But the Celts of Gaul, the people of the modern kingdom of France, have held one of the first places in Europe by help of what they learned, first from Roman and then from Teutonic conquerors. And, as the Celts came too soon, so the Slaves came too late. They have formed several powerful nations, yet they have never taken the lead in the way that the Greeks, Romans, and Teutons have done. Our history then will mainly be a history of the way in which the Roman dominion came together, and of the way in which it fell asunder.

9. **Things common to all the European Nations.**—If the Aryan people ever were mere savages, that time had passed away before they came into Europe. They had already made some way in the most needful arts, and all of them had much the same original form of government. As families and clans grew into tribes, and as tribes grew into nations, each tribe or nation had a king or chief of some kind, a council of elders or nobles, and a general assembly of the whole people. And there was commonly a three-fold distinction between the nobles by birth, the common freemen, and their slaves or bondmen. Out of these elements, all modern European society has grown up. The old Aryans had also a common religion, which took different forms among different nations, but in all of which many gods were worshipped, the chief gods having been at first the great powers of nature, as the sky and the sun. Afterwards Christianity became the religion of the Roman Empire, and spread gradually over all Europe; but it took somewhat different forms in eastern and western, in northern and southern, Europe. But for many ages past, all the people of Europe have been Christians of some kind, except perhaps a few non-Aryan people in the extreme north, and also except the Mahometans who in some

parts have come in as conquerors. This they did in Spain and Sicily, whence they have been driven out, and in south-eastern Europe, where they still abide.

10. **Summary.**—Europe then is a continent consisting of three main parts, Southern, Central, and Northern. Of these, the southern part consists of the islands and peninsulas of the Mediterranean Sea, among which the history of civilized man begins. Of the great families of mankind, those which concern us are the Aryan, the Semitic, and the others whom we may call non-Aryan. Successive swarms of Aryan nations have gradually settled in Europe, destroying the older people or driving them into corners. These Aryan nations had all once been one people, and they still showed signs of having been one people in their language, their religion, and their laws and manners. Among the nations, three, the Greeks, the Romans, and the Teutons, have, one after another, held the chief place. Among these again, the Romans at one time united under their power all the nations round the Mediterranean Sea, and European history is chiefly made up of the way in which their dominion came together and broke asunder. Lastly, all the Aryan nations of Europe gradually embraced the Christian religion, though that religion took different forms in different countries.

CHAPTER II.

THE GREEKS.

1. **Greece and the Greek People.**—As Europe has more inland seas, islands, and peninsulas than any other part of the old world, so Greece has more inland seas, islands, and peninsulas than any other part of Europe. It is also a very mountainous land,

so that the whole of Greece is made up of peninsulas, islands, and valleys, cut off from one another either by the sea or by the mountains. Thus the men who dwelled in that land could hardly fail to become a sea-faring folk, and to plant colonies in other lands. They were also sure not to join under one government, but to keep apart in small states, each town or district being, or trying to be, independent of all others. And, though no part of Greece is very far from the sea, yet some parts are more inland, and some parts are still fuller of islands and peninsulas, than others; and it was in the parts of Greece which lay nearest to the sea that the most famous Greek cities arose. And from the sea-faring parts of Greece men went forth who planted Greek colonies, some in the neighbouring islands, and some at more distant points round a large part of the coast of the Mediterranean Sea. The name which the Greeks called themselves, was **Hellênes**, and wherever **Hellénes** dwelled was **Hêllas**. Thus there were patches of Hellas in many parts of the Mediterranean coasts, planted in the midst of other nations. But in Greece itself all was Hellas, and none but Hellênes dwelled there.

2. **Character of the Greeks.**—Now all these things, division into many small states, a sea-faring life, and all that such a life leads to, are things that greatly tend to sharpen the wits, and Greece was peopled by men who had more wits to sharpen than any other men. Another people in Greece might not have done such great things as the Greeks did; and the Greeks might not have done such great things in any other land. But the land and its people fitted one another, and so great things came of them. The Greeks had the start of all other people in literature and art and science, and, above all, in the art of government or politics. For they were the first people who made free commonwealths, and who

put the power of the law instead of mere force and the arbitrary will of a single man.

3. **Greeks and Barbarians.**—It is most likely that the Greeks and Italians, and several other nations of eastern Europe and western Asia, all belonged to the same great branch of the Aryan family. Anyhow the Greeks and Italians, the Sikels, who gave their name to the island of **Sicily**, the people to the north of Greece in **Epeiros** and **Macedonia**, and some of the people on the eastern coast of the Ægæan Sea, were all akin to each other. But the Greeks early shot ahead of all their kinsfolk, so that they looked upon the rest as **barbarians**. This word at first meant simply people whose language could not be understood, and the Greeks called all nations by that name. They even called men **barbarians** whose tongue was really very nearly akin to their own, if it had so parted off that they could no longer understand it. Afterwards the word came to carry with it a certain feeling of contempt and dislike; and in modern use it has a stronger meaning still. But, at first, it simply meant **not-Greek**. All mankind were either Hellênes or barbarians.

4. **The Phœnicians.**—Among the barbarian nations, the Greek colonies had to deal with men of all the different nations round the Mediterranean. The Greeks of old Greece had in Europe mainly to deal with the kindred nations who had not grown so fast as they had. Their first great barbarian rivals came from Asia. These were the **Phœnicians**, as the Greeks called them, but they called themselves **Canaanites**. They lived in Sidon and Tyre, and other cities on the Syrian coast, and they planted colonies in many parts of the Mediterranean before the Greeks did. The Greeks in earlier times drove them out of many of the islands of the Ægæan Sea; and in after times Greek and Phœnician colonies strove for the great islands of Sicily and

Cyprus. And it was from the Phœnicians that the Greeks learned the art of alphabetic writing, which the rest of Europe has learned from them. This is almost the only great gift which the Greeks got from any strangers. In everything else they wrought up the common stock of the Aryan family to greater perfection than any other people, and with less help from strangers.

5. **The Greek Colonies.**—When trustworthy history first begins, many Greek colonies had already been planted round a large part of the coast of the Mediterranean. But in some places the Phœnicians had got before the Greeks, and in others, as in central and northern Italy, the native people were too strong and brave to let any strangers settle among them. But Greek colonies were planted round the whole of the Ægæan and part of the Euxine Sea; in the lands and islands to the north-west of Greece; in Sicily and southern Italy; in Cyprus; in the part of Africa which lies between Egypt and the great Phœnician settlement of Carthage; and on the Mediterranean coasts of Gaul and Spain. But no Greeks ever dared to pass the **Pillars of Hêraklês**, that is, the Straits of Gibraltar, to plant colonies on the coasts of the Ocean. Many of these colonies, as **Milêtos** in Asia, **Sybaris** in Italy, **Syracuse** in Sicily, and **Massalia**, now **Marseilles**, in Gaul, were in early times among the greatest cities of the Greek zone. They everywhere spread the Greek tongue, and somewhat of Greek manners, among the people around them. The colonies on the western coast of Asia were among the oldest and most famous of all, and the story of the War of Troy, as sung by **Homer**, is most likely a legendary account of the Greek settlements in those lands.

6. **The Legendary Times of Greece.**—We learn something of the state of Greece in very early times from the poems of Homer. In those days the **Greeks** had already made some progress in the

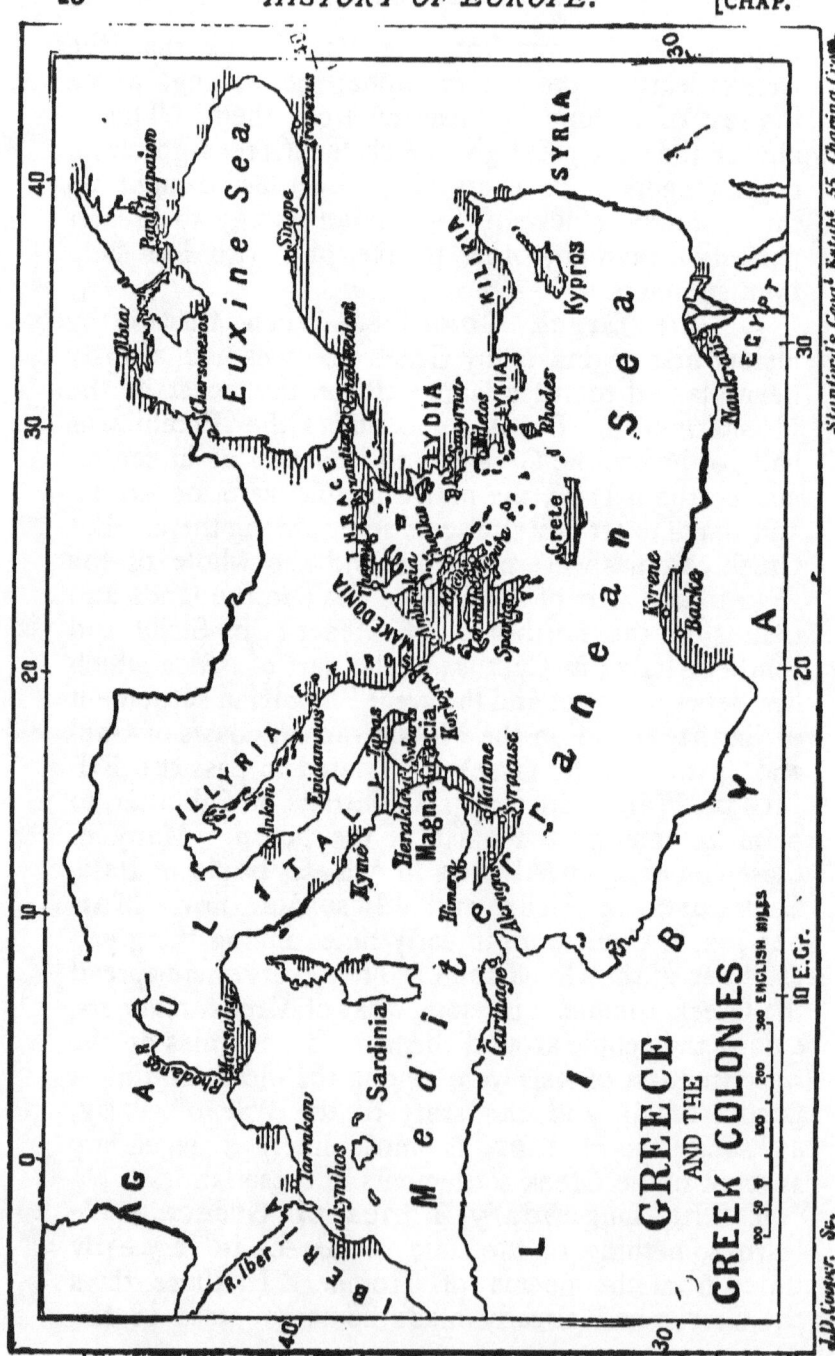

arts, and they had formed governments of the kind common to all the Aryan nations. Each city or other small district had its king, with a council of elders or nobles, and an assembly of the people. But before historic times begin, kings were put aside in most Greek cities, and the power had come into the hands of the nobles. In early Greece also the geographical divisions, and the degree of power held by different cities, were quite unlike what they were afterwards. The catalogue of the Greek forces in Homer gives us a kind of map of legendary Greece, which is quite unlike anything in historical Greece. Thus, in the north of Greece, **Thessaly** was of much more importance than it was afterwards. Thus in **Peloponnêsos** the chief power was at **Mykênê**, a city which in later times had no power at all. **Agamemnôn**, King of Mykênê, is described as the commander of the whole Greek force; and in those early times his people, the **Achaians**, were certainly the head people of Peloponnêsos and of all Greece, and Mykênê was their chief city. The southern islands of the Ægæan were already Greek, but no part of the coast of Asia. The poems describe the beginning of the Greek settlements there.

7. **The Dorian Migration.**—This state of things was greatly changed shortly before trustworthy history begins. For the **Dorians**, hitherto a small people of northern Greece, invaded Peloponnêsos and occupied its chief cities. From this time the Dorian cities, first **Argos** and then **Sparta**, were the leading powers of Peloponnêsos, and for a time of all Greece. The greatness of **Athens** came later; and for some ages the cities of old Greece were less great and flourishing than many of the Greek colonies, though the greatness of the cities in old Greece, when it came lasted longer.

8. **The Greek Commonwealths.**—When the kingly power was abolished in the Greek cities, they

became republics or commonwealths. Sometimes a priest or magistrate kept the title of king, but he was no longer the head of the state. But at Sparta the kings went on, two kings at a time, the kingdom in each line going on from father to son. But though the Spartan kings were held in high honour, and commanded armies and had various powers of other kinds, still they ceased, step by step, to be the real heads of the state. This doing away with kings was one of the chief things which distinguished the Greeks in Greece from their neighbours and kinsfolk; for in Macedonia and Epeiros, and in some of the Greek islands and colonies, kings went on after they had come to an end in Greece itself.

9. **Aristocracies and Democracies.** — The governments which were now formed were for the most part **aristocracies** or **oligarchies**, that is to say, governments in which the power is in the hands of some particular class of the people. Such a government, if it ruled well, the Greeks called **aristocracy** or government of the **best**; and, if it ruled badly, an **oligarchy** or government of the **few**. The aristocracy or oligarchy was commonly made up of the old citizens, who did not allow those who settled afterwards to have the same rights as themselves. Some cities always remained oligarchies; but in others the new citizens or commons were able to get the power placed in the hands of all citizens without distinction. This was called a **democracy** or government of the whole people. And sometimes, when strifes of this kind were going on in a city, a cunning man was able, most commonly by pretending to help the commons, to get all power into his own hands. Such an one was called a **Tyrant**, that is to say, one who had got the power, or more than the power, of a king, in a state where there was no king by law. The Greeks held that **monarchy**, where the chief power is in the hands of a king,

FORMS OF GOVERNMENT.

aristocracy, where it is in the hands of part only of the people, and **democracy**, where it is in the hands of the whole people, were all lawful forms of government. But **tyranny** was always held to be something in itself, and it was thought a good work to kill a tyrant. Of the aristocratic states Sparta was the greatest; for, though Sparta had kings, yet the chief power was in the hands of a few senators and magistrates, who were chosen from the old citizens only. Athens, on the other hand, was the great example of a democracy where every free citizen had a vote in the assembly which chose magistrates and made war and peace.

10. **Ruling and Subject Cities.**—It must be remembered that every Greek city was, or wished to be, an independent state, with the power of making war and peace. But very often one city bore rule over other cities, which were commonly eager to cast off its yoke if they could. Thus Sparta ruled over a large part of Peloponnêsos, having many smaller towns as her subjects. In Attica, on the other hand, the free citizens of all the towns had equal rights with those who lived in Athens. But Athens too, in after times, began to make subjects in other parts of Greece.

11. **The Greek Nation.**—As the Greeks were thus divided into many separate commonwealths, and scattered over distant parts of the world, they did not form one nation in the sense in which the great kingdoms and commonwealths of modern Europe do. Yet there was much to bind all Greeks everywhere together, and to make them feel themselves one people as compared with the rest of the world. They spoke one language; for, though the Greek tongue was not spoken everywhere in exactly the same way, yet all Greeks everywhere could understand one another. They worshipped the same gods; there were common games in honour of those gods, in which every

Greek, and none but Greeks, might take a part; and all Greeks all over the world had many customs in common. They had a common possession in the songs of Homer and other poets; and they gradually began to feel that they were above other nations in literature and art. Thus the distinction between Greeks and barbarians grew wider; and, though the Greeks were always fighting against one another, yet it was commonly thought shameful to let any Greeks fall under the power of barbarians. At last, towards the beginning of the fifth century before Christ, the Greeks of old Greece were driven to act together as they had never done before when their country was invaded by a barbarian king.

12. **The Persian Wars.**—We have said that the Greek colonies were not able to keep their freedom so long as the cities of old Greece. This was first shown in the case of the Greeks on the east coast of the Ægæan. In the course of the sixth century before Christ, **Crœsus**, king of **Lydia**, conquered the Greek cities in his neighbourhood. The Lydian kingdom was soon after conquered by **Cyrus**, king of **Persia**, and now the Persians got possession of the Greek cities in Asia. Thus the two great branches of the Aryan family, eastern and western, which had been so long parted, now met again as enemies; for the Persians were really kinsfolk of the Greeks, though neither Greeks nor Persians knew of it. The first city of old Greece which had any war with the Persians was Athens. Athens was now a democracy, and had lately driven out its Tyrant, **Hippias** the son of **Peisistratos**. The Greeks of Asia and Cyprus now tried to throw off the Persian yoke; the Athenians gave them help, and so made the Persian kings their enemies. In 490 B.C., the Persian king **Darius** sent an army against Athens, which the Athenians, under **Miltiades**, defeated at **Marathôn**, with no help except from the little city of **Plataia**. In 480

B.C., Xerxes, the son of Darius, himself came into Greece with a much greater force by sea and land. All the lands through which he passed in Thrace and Macedonia submitted to him, and so did a great part of Greece itself. But Athens, Sparta, and many other Greek cities, withstood the Persians manfully both by sea and land. Then were fought the battles of **Thermopylai**, where **Leônidas**, the Spartan king, was killed; of **Salamis**, where we hear of the famous Athenian **Themistoklês**, of **Plataia**, and of **Mýkalê**. The Persians were thus driven out of Greece for ever, and for a while also out of all the lands round the Ægæan, till the quarrels of the Greeks allowed the barbarians again to get power at their cost.

13. **The Peloponnesian War.**—This came about through a quarrel between Athens and Sparta. Athens was now stronger by sea than any other Greek city; and her ships had done most to win the battle of Salamis. Therefore, when the Persians were driven out of Greece, many of the Greek islands and sea-faring towns in Thrace and Asia made an alliance with Athens at their head, in order to keep the Persians out of all Greek lands everywhere. But step by step Athens changed from being merely the head of all these cities to being their mistress, and she began to treat her allies as subjects. This was the time when Athens, under her great leader **Periklês**, was at the height of her glory, when her great temples were built, and the plays of her great poets were acted in her theatres. But this greatness of Athens raised up jealousy and hatred against her, and quarrels arose between her and the cities which were allied with Sparta, especially with **Corinth** and **Thebes**. Thus in 431 B.C. there broke out a war between Sparta and her allies on one side, and Athens and her allies and subjects on the other. As nearly all the Peloponnesian states were joined together

against Athens, this war is called the **Peloponnesian War**. With a short interval of peace this war went on for twenty-seven years by land and by sea. In 415 B.C. Athens attacked **Syracuse** in Sicily, on which the Spartans helped the Syracusans, and the Athenian enterprise came to nothing. Then the allies of Athens began to revolt, and the Persians began to step in again. At last, in 404 B.C., Athens had to surrender to the Spartan **Lysandros**. She now lost all her dominion over other cities, and had to change her democracy for an oligarchy of Thirty. But in the very next year Athens got back her freedom, though not her old dominion.

14. **Greek Writers and Philosophers.**—During the Peloponnesian war we first begin to get the help of historians who lived at the time, and who sometimes had themselves a share in the events which they wrote about. The history of the Persian war was written by **Herodotus**, who had talked with men who had themselves seen what he records. But the history of the early part of the Peloponnesian war was written by **Thucydides**, who not only lived at the time, but himself bore a part in the war. And the history of the latter part of the Peloponnesian war, and of the wars which follow, was written by **Xenophón**, who also had a hand in much that he wrote about. He served along with many other Greeks, who were not sent by any Greek city but served for pay, in an attempt of the Persian prince **Cyrus** to make himself king instead of his brother **Artaxerxes**. This attempt failed; but the return of the Greeks who helped Cyrus is very famous by the name of the **Retreat of the Ten Thousand**. Xenophôn was the pupil of the philosopher **Sokrates**, who wrote nothing, but who made a great name by his private talk, and was at last put to death by the Athenians. The time of the Peloponnesian war was also the time of the great dramatic

poets of Athens, Æschylus, Sophoklês, Euripidês, and Aristophanês.

15. **Sparta and Thebes.**—Sparta was now at the head of Greece, and her rule was far harder than the rule of Athens had ever been; so wars were soon stirred up against her. The first was with her old enemy Athens, helped by her old allies Corinth and Thebes. The Persians helped first one side and then the other, and this war was ended by the Peace of **Antalkidas**, by which all the Greek cities of Asia were once more given up to the Persian king. Sparta was now more powerful than ever, and treacherously seized the citadel of Thebes in time of peace. But the Thebans presently got their freedom again, and under two great leaders **Pelopidas** and **Epameinôndas**, Thebes became for a while the chief city of Greece. Epameinôndas even invaded Peloponnêsos and founded two new cities, **Messênê** and **Megalopolis**. He was killed in the battle of **Mantineia** in 362; and now all the chief cities were so weakened by this endless fighting that another power was ready to step in.

16. **The Rise of Macedonia.**—The people of Macedonia, the country to the north-east of Greece, were no doubt akin to the Greeks, but they were counted as barbarians. But their kings were Greeks from Argos, and they did much to bring in Greek ways among their people. The time now came when Macedonia was to meddle in Greek affairs, to be acknowledged as a Greek state, and to win the chief power in Greece, such as Sparta and other cities had held at different times. The Spartans themselves opened a way for the Macedonian kings by destroying a league which the Greek city of **Olynthos** in their neighbourhood had begun to form, and which would have been a great check on their power. By this time Sparta, Athens, and Thebes, were all weakened by their wars, and Macedonia was ruled by a

very able and enterprising king called **Philip**. He first stepped in by professing to defend the temple of Apollo at **Delphoi** which had been robbed by the **Phokians**. Then he had wars with the Athenians and Thebans, whom he overthrew in the battle of **Chairôneia** in 338, and after that he was acknowledged as chief captain of Greece to make war upon Persia. But just as he was setting out, he was murdered by one of his own subjects. This was the time of the great Greek orators, and it was in calling on the Athenians to war against Philip that **Dêmosthenês**, the greatest of them, won his fame.

17. **Alexander the Great.**—The war against Persia, which Philip had designed, was carried out by his son **Alexander**. He gave out that he wished to revenge the wrongs which the old Persian kings had done to Macedonia and Greece. In 334 he set forth, and in three years he conquered the Persian empire, winning the three great battles of **Granikos**, **Issos**, and **Arbêla**. He went exploring and conquering as far as India, and in 323 he died at Babylon, having never come back to Macedonia or Greece. Alexander was the greatest of all conquerors, and his conquests carried the Greek tongue and Greek art and manners over a large part of the world. His great dominion could not hold together; but, when it was divided among his generals, the Macedonian kings everywhere made Greek the chief language of their dominions, and founded Greek cities everywhere. Thus **Alexandria** in Egypt, founded by Alexander himself, **Antioch** in Syria, and other cities founded by his successors, were reckoned amongst the greatest Greek cities.

18. **The Successors of Alexander.**—Of the Macedonian kingdoms which arose out of the division of the empire of Alexander, the greatest was the kingdom of **Seleukos** and his descendants. This at one time stretched from the Ægæan to India, but It

afterwards shrank up into a mere kingdom of **Syria**. But Greece had more to do with the kings of Egypt, the **Ptolemies**, who were great patrons of Greek literature in their own capital of Alexandria, and who for a good while held several islands and other points in the Ægæan. The kings of **Pergamos**, who were also great patrons of literature, had also much to do with Greek affairs, and the immediate neighbours the kings who ruled in Macedonia itself, had more still. These were the descendants of **Antigonos**, one of Alexander's generals, and his son **Dêmêtrios** called **Poliorkêtês** or the **Besieger**. This dynasty began about 294, after a time of great confusion. Epeiros began to be a great power under its king **Pyrrhos**, who died in 272. The Macedonian kings now held Thessaly and other parts of northern Greece almost as parts of their own kingdom, and there were many other Greek cities in which they had garrisons, or which were ruled by tyrants under their influence.

19. **The Achaian and Ætolian Leagues.**—In the later times of Grecian history the chief power was in quite other hands from those in which it was in the times of the Persian and Peloponnêsian wars. Athens and Thebes were now of very little account; Sparta looked up a good deal under her kings **Agis** and **Kleomenês**, but the chief states of Greece in this later time were the two leagues of **Achaia** and **Ætolia**. The Achaians, who had once been so great, now held only the cities on the north coast of Peloponnêsos, and it was among them that the league began. The Greek cities had now found that they could not withstand the Macedonian kings as long as each city stood quite by itself, so they began to join together in leagues or **confederations**. That is to say, several cities joined together, each still settling its own affairs at home, but all acting together as one state in matters of peace and war. The example

spread so that the people of Epeiros put away their kings and made themselves a league of commonwealths, and even in Asia the cities of **Lykia** joined themselves together into a league after the Greek fashion and kept themselves independent. And some other out-lying Greek states, as the **Cretan** cities, the island of **Rhodes**, and the city of **Byzantion**, kept themselves independent of all the kings. In old Greece the business of the leagues was to preserve their freedom and win back that of other cities from the kings of Macedonia. The Achaian League began about 280, and grew step by step till at last it took in all Peloponnêsos. The League, under its general Aratos, set free many cities from Macedonia; yet at last in 223, when the Achaians were hard pressed in a war with Kleomenês of Sparta, Aratos was so unwise as to make an alliance with **Antigonos**, king of Macedonia. After this time, the League was never so strong and independent as it had been before; and now the Romans began to meddle with Greek affairs till they brought all Greece and Macedonia under their power.

20. **Summary.**—The great value of the history of Greece is because it is the history of the world in a small space. There is no lesson which history teaches us which we cannot learn from Grecian history. And this is mainly because in Greece everything, whether forms of government, literature, art, or philosophy, is all quite fresh and not borrowed from any other people. In all these ways Greece, though so small a part of the world, has influenced all the history of the world ever since. But Greece has very largely done this by influencing Rome. It is with Rome that the unbroken history of Europe begins, and of this we will go on to speak in the next chapter.

CHAPTER III.

THE GROWTH OF ROME.

1. **The Peninsula of Italy.**—We have already said that Rome became the centre of all European history. The position of Rome greatly helped it in so doing; for, of the three great peninsulas, Italy is the central one, and Rome is nearly in the centre of Italy. The name Italy has not always had the same meaning. In this chapter it will mean the middle peninsula of Europe in the strictest sense, not taking in all the lands as far as the Alps, but only the peninsula itself. What is now Northern Italy was not yet Italian. The peninsula itself is by no means so broken up by gulfs and promontories as Greece is, nor has it so many islands lying along its shores. Italy then did not begin to play its part in history so early as Greece did; it was not so completely cut up into small states as Greece was, nor were its people given to a seafaring and colonizing life like the Greeks. The business of Greece in the world's history was to teach mankind; that of Italy, through its chief city Rome, was to conquer mankind and to give them laws. Of the three great islands near Italy, Sicily alone plays a great part both in Greek and in Italian history. And the southern part of Italy, near Sicily, has a coast much more broken up, like a Greek coast, than the rest of Italy. Great things came of this difference.

2. **The Inhabitants of Italy.**—The greater part of Italy was, when we begin to learn anything about it, held by a branch of the Aryan family, who were more closely akin to the Greeks than to any other of the kindred races. This race we may call **Italians, and they may be grouped into two great**

classes, the **Oscan** and the **Latin**. The Oscans, including under that name the Umbrians, Sabellians, and other tribes, we first hear of on the Hadriatic side of Italy, and the Latins on the Mediterranean side. Besides these, in the north-west of the peninsula, were the **Etruscans**, a people of very doubtful origin. Some have thought that they were not Aryans at all, just as the **Ligurians**, who bordered on the peninsula to the north-west, were most likely not Aryan but akin to the Basques. The rest of what is now Northern Italy was mostly held by Celtic tribes, and was reckoned for a part of Gaul. In the extreme north-east were the **Venetians**, a people of uncertain origin. In Sicily were the **Sikanians**, who seem to have been akin to the Ligurians, and the **Sikels**, an Italian people allied to the Latins. Moreover in Southern Italy and in Sicily there were many Greek colonies, and in Sicily there were Phœnician colonies also. The earliest history of Italy is chiefly made up, first of the way in which the Oscan nations pressed both upon the Latins and upon the Greek colonies, and secondly of the way in which all came under the power of the one Latin city of Rome.

3. **The Beginning of Rome.**—As Rome came in the end to be the head of Italy and the world, there grew up in after times many tales about the beginning of the city. It was said that Rome was founded by a man named **Romulus**, who was suckled by a wolf. Such stories are told of the founders of other cities, and no scholar now believes them, though they are pretty enough to read as tales. Rome really grew out of several towns on the hills near the Tiber, the oldest of which was the Latin town on the **Palatine**. Most of the other hills were held by Latins; but one, the **Capitoline** hill, was **Sabine**. As the hills were so near together, these towns were gradually made into one city. Rome grew in all ages

by admitting her allies or subjects to her citizenship, and we thus see that she did this from the beginning. But the new citizens did not always get their full rights all at once. Thus there grew up at Rome a distinction between the **Patricians**—that is the old citizens, the descendants of the first settlers —and the **Plebeians**, the descendants of those who came in afterwards. The struggles between the Plebeians, who strove to get the same rights as the Patricians, and the Patricians, who wanted to keep all power in their own hands, make up a great part of the history of Rome.

4. **The Kings of Rome.**—Legend says that there were seven kings of Rome, and gives us their names. We cannot be certain as to their number, and, though the later kings of Rome may be real persons, the earlier ones are certainly fabulous. But no doubt there were kings in Rome, and it is quite likely that, for some while after the two towns on the Palatine and Capitoline hills became one city, the king was chosen from each in turn. For at Rome the kingdom did not go from father to son, as it did in the Greek states. As among other Aryan states, there was beside the king a Senate and an Assembly of the people. The people were at first only the Patricians or old citizens; but, when the Plebeians had won equal rights with the Patricians, the Roman People meant the Patricians and the Plebeians both together. Under her later kings Rome became a powerful state. The seven hills were fenced in by one wall, and the city bore rule over all Latium. At last, about the time when Hippias was driven out of Athens, kingship was put away, because, so the story says, of the wickedness of the last king **Lucius Tarquinius** and his son. The powers of the king were given to two magistrates chosen for a year, who were called first **Prætors** and then **Consuls**. They were at first chosen from among the Patricians only, and one of

the great disputes between the two orders was the claim of the Plebeians to have one consul chosen from among them.

5. **The Roman Conquest of Italy.**—When Rome had driven out her kings, she no longer kept her power over the Latins, and she was much pressed by the Etruscans beyond the Tiber. But the Oscan nations, especially the **Æquians** and **Volscians**, were now pressing on the Latins, and Rome and Latium were glad to become equal allies. For a long time too Rome was weakened by the quarrel between the Patricians and Plebeians. But at last, about B.C. 396, the Romans gained a footing beyond the Tiber by taking the Etruscan city of **Veii**. Six years after this, the Gauls from beyond the Po pressed down into Central Italy, and Rome was taken and burned by them. Presently the two orders grew closer together; and in 366, there was, for the first time, a Plebeian Consul, Lucius Sextius. From this time Rome was much stronger, and began to conquer Italy in good earnest. From 343 to 290 there were wars between the Romans and the **Samnites**, who had made themselves the chief power in Southern Italy, at the expense of both Italians and Greeks. And, between these Samnite wars, Rome got back her old power over her kinsfolk the Latins. In the latter part of the Samnite wars Rome had to fight against the Etruscans and Gauls as well as the Samnites; but in the end she got the better of all, and by the year 282 all the states of Italy had become her allies, except some of the Greek cities in the south.

6. **The Roman Dominion in Italy.**—The dominion of Rome over her Italian **Allies** was of the same kind as when one city in Greece bore rule over another. The conquered city still remained a separate state with its own government, but it had to obey the Romans and follow their lead in war. But some parts of Italy were better off than the Allies, for the Romans

gave the full franchise of their own city to many of their neighbours in a way that the Greek cities hardly ever did. And others got the **Latin** franchise, that is, the rights which were left to the Latin cities on their conquest. These Latins could in certain cases claim Roman citizenship as a right, which the Italians could not. Thus there were three classes among the free inhabitants of Italy, **Romans, Latins,** and **Italians or Allies**; and it was promotion for an Italian to become a Latin, and for a Latin to become a Roman.

7. **The War with Pyrrhos.**—Now that Rome was mistress of Italy, she had presently to struggle with foreign enemies. The freedom of Greece was now quite crushed under Macedonia, but the Macedonian conquests had made Greek arts and arms more famous than ever. The Greeks in Italy and Sicily, threatened and partly conquered by the Romans and Carthaginians, sought help from old Greece against the barbarians; so **Pyrrhos**, king of Epeiros, which was now reckoned as a Greek state, came over to help the Greek city of **Taras** or **Tarentum** against the Romans. As the Romans were not used to the Greek manner of fighting, he defeated them in two battles, but in a third he was defeated himself, and he went back to Greece in B.C. 276, leaving the Romans to conquer the small part of Italy which was left. This was the beginning of the wars which Rome, as the head of Italy, now waged with other nations, and which gave her her great foreign dominion.

8. **The Punic Wars.**—But, before Rome made further conquests in Europe, she had to deal with an enemy in Africa. The great Phœnician city of **Carthage** now was the head of several Phœnician colonies on the coasts of Africa and Spain. The Carthaginians were a sea-faring and trading people, and they made settlements in Sicily and the other islands of the western Mediterranean, just as the other Phœnicians had done in Cyprus and the other eastern islands,

Rome and Carthage were now the two great powers of the West. Rome was strong by land, and Carthage by sea: Rome fought by the arms of her own citizens and allies, and Carthage chiefly by hired soldiers. As Sicily lay between them, they soon began to quarrel about Sicilian affairs. Then came the **Punic Wars**, a struggle for the dominion of the West between a Semitic and an Aryan power. The first Punic war lasted from B.C. 264 to 241, when Carthage gave up to Rome her dominions in Sicily. To make up for this, the Carthaginians under **Hamilcar** gained a great dominion in Spain, and in B.C. 218, the second Punic war began, which is also called the **Hannibalian War**, from Hamilcar's son **Hannibal**, the greatest man that Carthage ever had, and one of the greatest in the history of the world. He entered Italy by land, defeated the Romans in several battles, and persuaded many of their allies to revolt. But meanwhile the Roman general **Publius Cornelius Scipio** conquered the Carthaginian possessions in Spain, and carried the war into Africa. So, after many years, Hannibal had to go back to defend Carthage, and he was defeated at **Zama** in B.C. 202. Carthage had to give up a large territory to Massinissa, king of Numidia, who was an ally of Rome, and had herself to become a dependent ally of Rome.

9. **The Roman Provinces.**—These wars with Carthage gave Rome a new kind of dominion, namely the **Provinces**, or lands which she held out of Italy. While the Italian states, though bound to follow the lead of Rome, were still separate states, managing their own internal affairs, the provinces had to pay tribute to Rome and were put under Roman governors. But particular cities and districts were often left with the name of free allies, and they were sometimes rewarded with the Italian, the Latin, or even the Roman franchise. The first Roman Province was **Sicily.** Soon after the end of the first Punic war,

Rome made new provinces of **Sardinia** and **Corsica**, and presently of the Carthaginian dominions in **Spain**. But some particular cities were left free. Thus **Gades** or **Cadiz**, the great Phœnician city on the Ocean, which had been a rival of Carthage and a friend of Rome, was always counted a free ally, and in the end it got full Roman citizenship. So was the Greek city of **Massalia** in Gaul, and other places here and there. Still, though Gades and Massalia were quite free as to their internal government, they would not have dared to make war or peace against the will of Rome.

10. **The Macedonian Wars.**—The third great power in Europe, besides Rome and Carthage, was **Macedonia**, which soon got mixed up in their quarrels. Between the first and second Punic war, the Romans had a war with Illyria, and some of the Greek colonies on the Illyrian coast called in the Romans as deliverers. The Romans thus got a footing on that side of the Hadriatic, and began to be looked to as friends by most of the Greek states. But when any people had anything to do with Rome, either in peace or in war, they were sure, first to become dependent allies, and in the end to be made into provinces. Thus it was with Carthage, with Macedonia, and with all Greece. In B.C. 215, the Macedonian king **Philip** made a league with Hannibal, which of course led to a war with Rome, which lasted from 213 to 205. The Achaian League and some other of the Greek states helped Macedonia; the Ætolian League helped Rome, as did King Attalos of Pergamos, her first ally beyond the Ægæan. This war led only to a slight change of frontier; but the Romans now began steadily to meddle in Greek affairs. In B.C. 200 the Romans helped Athens against Macedonia, and a second war began. The Ætolian League at first, and the Achaian League afterwards, helped the Romans. In 197 Philip was

defeated at **Kynoskephalê**, and all that part of Greece which had been under his dominion was declared free. Macedonia now became a dependent ally of Rome, and the other Greek states, though free in name, became really dependent.

11. **The Syrian War.**—In Roman history one war and one conquest always led to another. The Ætolians now thought that they had not gained enough by their alliance with Rome; so they asked **Antiochos** king of Syria to come over and attack the Romans in Europe. He was of the house of **Seleukos**; but the great Seleukid kingdom had been cut short in the East about B.C. 256, by the revolt of the **Parthians** under **Arsakes**, who founded a kingdom which afterwards became the chief rival of Rome. But the Seleukid dominion still stretched beyond the Tigris, and its capital Antioch was one of the greatest Greek cities. But in Asia Minor the Ptolemies of Egypt still held part of the south coast, and there were still some independent states, like the kingdoms of **Pergamos** and **Bithynia**, and the cities of **Hêrakleia** and **Sinôpê**. In this war the chief allies of Rome were the Achaians in Europe, and Eumenês of Pergamos in Asia. Antiochos was defeated in two battles, at **Thermopylai** and at **Magnêsia** in Asia. Then he gave up all his lands west of Mount Tauros, most of which was given to Eumenês. The Achaians were allowed to join all Peloponnêsos to their League, while Ætolia became a Roman dependency. Rome had taken to herself the islands of **Zakynthos** and **Kephallênia**. But she now became really mistress both of Greece and of Western Asia, for her alliance was only a step towards subjection.

12. **The Roman Conquests in the West.** —The wars with Carthage, Macedonia, and Syria made Rome the chief power throughout the Mediterranean lands. Only a small part had been brought under her dominion; but there was no longer any free

state which could meet her on equal terms. All the older powers, Phœnician and Greek as well as Italian, had become practically dependent. But Rome had still to establish her power over the barbarian nations of the West, to bring the dependent states under her complete dominion, and lastly, to struggle with those Eastern powers which now were her only rivals. The first work began as soon as Italy was conquered, for Italy was not safe without that part of Gaul which lay on the Italian side of the Alps. Rome was checked in this quarter by the Punic wars, during which the Gauls gave great help to Hannibal. But after the peace, the conquest of **Cisalpine Gaul** went on, and it was completed by B.C. 191. Meanwhile, by B.C. 133, when Numantia was taken, all Spain, except some of the wild parts in the north, was conquered. Then in B.C. 125 a province was made in **Transalpine Gaul**. Here the Romans stepped in to help Massalia against her Gaulish neighbours. This led to their making conquests for themselves: and before long all south-eastern Gaul was won. It was called the **Province**, to distinguish it from independent Gaul, and part of the land is still called **Provence**.

13. **The Final Conquest of Macedonia and Carthage.** — The second Punic and the second Macedonian war had changed the two rivals of Rome into her dependencies. But both Macedonia and Carthage were ready to throw off the yoke whenever they could. There was a third Macedonian war from 171 to 178, when the last king **Perseus** was defeated at **Pydna** by Lucius Æmilius Paullus. Macedonia was now cut up into four commonwealths; Epeiros was conquered and wasted, and the Romans were now masters of all Greece. A revolt in Macedonia in 149 ended in the country being made into a province. Then came a war with the Achaian League, and in B.C. 146 Corinth was destroyed and the League

was broken up. Greece was not yet made a province, and several Greek states were still called free, but all were practically subject. Meanwhile a third Punic war broke out, because the Romans abetted their allies in Africa against Carthage. In 146 Carthage was taken and destroyed by the younger Scipio. Thus two of the greatest sea-faring cities of the world were destroyed in one year. The Romans now made a province of **Africa** out of part of the territory of Carthage. Massinissa of Numidia got another part, but the time of bondage was to come for Numidia also. In 106, after a war with its king Jugurtha, Numidia became dependent on Rome, and a hundred years after the fall of Carthage it became a subject province.

14. **Disputes at Rome.**—Rome was now mistress all round the Mediterranean. The only great state with which she had had no war was **Egypt**, where the **Ptolemies**, the descendants of the first Ptolemy, reigned, and where Alexandria was one of the greatest of Greek cities. But even Egypt had begun to look to Rome as a protector. This great dominion abroad led to much corruption at home, for the old constitution of the one Roman city was not fitted for a state ruling over so great a part of the world. The provincials were mere subjects, and the allies had no voice in anything beyond their own internal affairs ; the Senate and People of Rome bore rule over both, and thus both were often greatly oppressed. Meanwhile the old struggles between patricians and plebeians had come to an end, and a much worse kind of quarrel, between rich and poor, was beginning. Those plebeians whose forefathers had held high magistracies were now counted as noble, as well as the patricians. Moreover all kinds of people, strangers and freedmen, that is, men who had been slaves, were made citizens. Thus the Roman people changed greatly ; the assembly became too large, and

sank into a mob. Then, while many citizens were wretchedly poor, others held great estates of common land against the law. The cause of the poor was taken up by **Tiberius Sempronius Gracchus** in 133, and by his brother **Caius** in 125. They passed laws to stop these evils; but their laws were never fully carried out, and they were themselves killed by those who wished to keep everything in their own hands.

15. **The Social War.**—Another source of dispute was soon mixed up with these internal quarrels. The Italian allies, who had helped Rome in all her conquests, began to ask for full citizenship. Caius Gracchus supported their claims, and afterwards **Caius Marius.** Marius had got great fame by ending the war with Jugurtha, and yet more by delivering Gaul from an invasion of the **Cimbri** and **Teutones.** These were people from the north, who were overthrown in 102 and 101 in two great battles at **Aquæ Sextiæ** or **Aix** in Transalpine, and at Vercellæ in Cisalpine, Gaul. Marius favoured the people against the nobles and the Italians against both the nobles and the Roman mob. But in the year 90 the allies (in Latin, Socii) revolted, and then began the **Social War.** Most of them submitted next year, and became Roman citizens, but the Samnites and Lucanians still went on fighting. In this war much fame was won by **Lucius Cornelius Sulla,** who became the head of the party of the nobles. Presently Marius and Sulla quarrelled, and the **Civil Wars** of Rome began. The Samnites now took the Marian side, and both Samnites and Marians were defeated by Sulla under the walls of Rome in the year 83. The Samnites meant to destroy Rome, but Sulla saved her, and so fixed the history of the whole world. Sulla then took the supreme power as **Perpetual Dictator,** but he presently gave up his office and died a private man. But with this giving one man all

power the overthrow of the Roman commonwealth began.

16. **Wars in Asia.**—Ever since the overthrow of Antiochos Rome had had great influence in Asia Minor, but she had no possessions there till in B.C. 133 **Attalos**, the last king of Pergamos, left his dominions to the Roman people. They were the first province beyond the Ægæan, that of **Asia**. This brought the Roman into the neighourhood of **Pontos**, the greatest native power in those parts. Under its king **Mithridatês** the Sixth or the Great, Pontos became very powerful, and from 88 to 63 Rome had a war with him greater than any war since the overthrow of Carthage and Macedonia. While the civil war was going on at Rome, Mithridatês won all Asia Minor, slew all the Romans and Italians who were settled there, and crossed over into Greece. In these wars the Roman generals were, first Sulla, then Lucius Licinius Lucullus, and lastly **Cnæus Pompeius**, who was called **Magnus** or the Great. In the end the kingdom of Pontos was overthrown **Armenia** was humbled, **Syria**, the last fragment of the great Seleukid kingdom, became a Roman province, and **Palestine** became a Roman dependency. The Roman power now reached the Euphrates, and Rome took the place of Greece and Macedonia as the champion of the West against the East. But this advance once more gave Rome a rival on equal terms in the kingdom of **Parthia**. In the year 54, a Roman army, under Marcus Licinius Crassus, went against Parthia, but he was utterly defeated and slain.

17. **The Civil War of Pompeius and Cæsar.**—Meanwhile it became more and more plain that one city was unfit to rule the world. There were constant disputes, and at last civil wars between the contending parties and the chief men of Rome. This was the time of the most famous men in

Roman history, such as, besides Pompeius and Crassus, the great orator **Marcus Tullius Cicero, Marcus Porcius Cato,** and **Caius Julius Cæsar.** Cæsar was a patrician, but, to serve his own purposes, he took up the cause of the people. In the year 58 he took the province of Gaul, and in about ten years he conquered the whole country. The Roman province of Gaul, instead of a small part in the south-west, now took in the whole land between the Pyrenees, the Rhine, and the Ocean. There were three chief nations in Gaul, the **Celts** in the middle, the **Aquitanians** in the south, who were akin to the Iberians, and those **German** tribes who lived west of the Rhine. Cæsar made expeditions both into the independent Germany beyond the Rhine, and into the isle of Britain. But he made no lasting conquests in either country. All this greatly strengthened his power, and, while he was away, things at Rome got into still greater confusion. In 49 Cæsar rebelled and invaded Italy. The great civil war now began between him and the armies of the Commonwealth under Pompeius. The war was in Greece, Spain, and Africa, and the chief battle was at **Pharsalos** in Thessaly where Pompeius was defeated. He then fled to Egypt, where he was murdered. Cæsar was now made Perpetual Dictator, and he was also called **Imperator,** that is General, a word which is cut short into **Emperor.** But, besides all this, he wanted to be king. Then many of the senators conspired, and slew him in the senate-house, March 15, B.C. 44.

18. **The Beginning of the Empire.**—After Cæsar's death, there was confusion for about thirteen years. Cæsar had adopted his great-nephew **Caius Octavius,** who thus became **Caius Julius Cæsar Octavianus.** He and **Marcus Antonius,** one of Cæsar's generals, waged war with the friends of the Commonwealth, whose chiefs were two of the men who had killed the elder Cæsar, **Caius Cassius**

and **Marcus Junius Brutus**. Cæsar, Antonius, and Marcus Æmilius Lepidus were made a **triumvirate** with all power in their hands. Then they overthrew Brutus and Cassius at the battle of **Philippi** in Macedonia, in 42. Antonius then set out against Parthia; but he stayed in Egypt with its queen **Kleopatra**, the last of the Ptolemies. Then came another civil war, in which Antonius and Kleopatra were defeated by Cæsar in a sea-fight at **Aktion** on the west coast of Greece, B.C. 31. Egypt now became a Roman province, and Cæsar became master of the state. The Senate and People voted him all kinds of honours and offices; but he took warning by the fate of his uncle, and did not call himself king or even dictator. From this time the old forms of the commonwealth went on, but the supreme power was always in the hands of one man. The chief of the State was called **Princeps** or **Prince**, and **Imperator** or **Emperor**, the title which prevailed in the end. Cæsar also received the new title of **Augustus**, and all who reigned after him, whether of his kin or not, always called themselves Cæsar and Augustus. But the first Emperor, Caius Julius Cæsar Octavianus, is known in history in a special way as Augustus Cæsar.

19. **The Roman Empire.**—The Roman state was thus changed from a commonwealth to a monarchy. But for a long time the Emperors had no royal pomp, but acted simply as chief magistrates of the commonwealth. Each Emperor was appointed by a vote of the Senate, which gave him such and such powers. The legions were kept up as a standing army, and the government rested more and more on the will of the soldiers. But now that all the Roman dominions were really subject to one man, the old distinctions of Romans, Latins, Italians, and Provincials gradually died out, till at last all the free inhabitants of the Roman Empire were declared to be

alike Romans. Rome thus changed from a city ruling over other lands into a mere seat of government for the whole empire. And a time came when the Emperors found that they were more wanted in cities nearer the frontier than they were at Rome. But for a long time after the empire began, no one would have said openly either that Rome had ceased to be still a commonwealth, or a ruling city.

20. **Extent of the Roman Empire.**—The conquest of Egypt gave Rome all the lands round the Mediterranean. Here and there a city or a principality was nominally free, but the Roman Emperor was really master everywhere. The conquests of Pompeius and the elder Cæsar had given Rome the Euphrates and the Rhine as frontiers, and before long it reached the Danube. This great dominion naturally fell into three parts. First there is **Western Europe**, Gaul and Spain, where the Romans were not only conquerors but civilizers, and where the Roman language and manners took root everywhere, except in out-of-the-way corners. To these we may add Africa, where Cæsar had restored Carthage as a Roman colony. Secondly, there are the lands from the Hadriatic to Mount Tauros, Greece and Asia Minor and the neighbouring lands, where the Roman language and manners could not displace the Greek civilization which had gradually spread since the time of Alexander. These may be called the **Greek** provinces. Thirdly, there are the **Eastern** provinces, the lands beyond Mount Tauros, as Syria and Egypt, where there were a few great Greek cities, but where neither Greek nor Latin could drive out the old language and the old manners.

21. **The Julian and Claudian Emperors.**— For nearly a hundred years the empire remained in the family of Augustus. That is, down to A.D. 68 all the Emperors were Cæsars by adoption, and most of them were really descendants of Augustus through

his daughter. These emperors were **Tiberius, Caius, Claudius, Nero**. All of these have left a bad name behind them, but Nero outdid all in wickedness. Under Augustus and Tiberius all the lands along the Danube were added to the empire, so that that river became the boundary like the Rhine and the Euphrates. Both Augustus and Tiberius made attempts to conquer Germany, which happily came to nothing. In the time of Augustus the German hero **Arminius** cut off a whole Roman army under Publius Quinctilius Varus. We English should remember that, if the Romans had conquered Germany, we should have been conquered too, as our forefathers were then still in their old homes in Northern Germany. The land where we now dwell, the isle of **Britain**, was then inhabited by a Celtic people, the Britons or Welsh. Britain was attacked by the Romans in the time of Claudius, and the greater part of it was gradually conquered and became a Roman province. But the northern part, as well as the neighbouring island of Ireland, was never conquered. Meanwhile several of the dependent kingdoms in Asia and Africa were made into provinces, and in the far east the kings of **Armenia** became vassals of Rome.

22. **The Empire at its Greatest Extent.**—After the death of Nero several Emperors were set up and put down in a very short time. Then came a long time of internal peace, under Emperors most of whom were very good rulers. First came the **Flavian** dynasty, that of **Titus Flavius Vespasianus** and his sons **Titus** and **Domitian**, of whom the last was the only thoroughly bad ruler of this time. Under Vespasian the Jews, who had revolted in the time of Nero, were conquered again, and **Jerusalem** was destroyed. After Domitian, from 96 to 180, ruled those who are called the five **Good Emperors, Nerva, Trajan, Hadrian, Antoninus Pius,** and

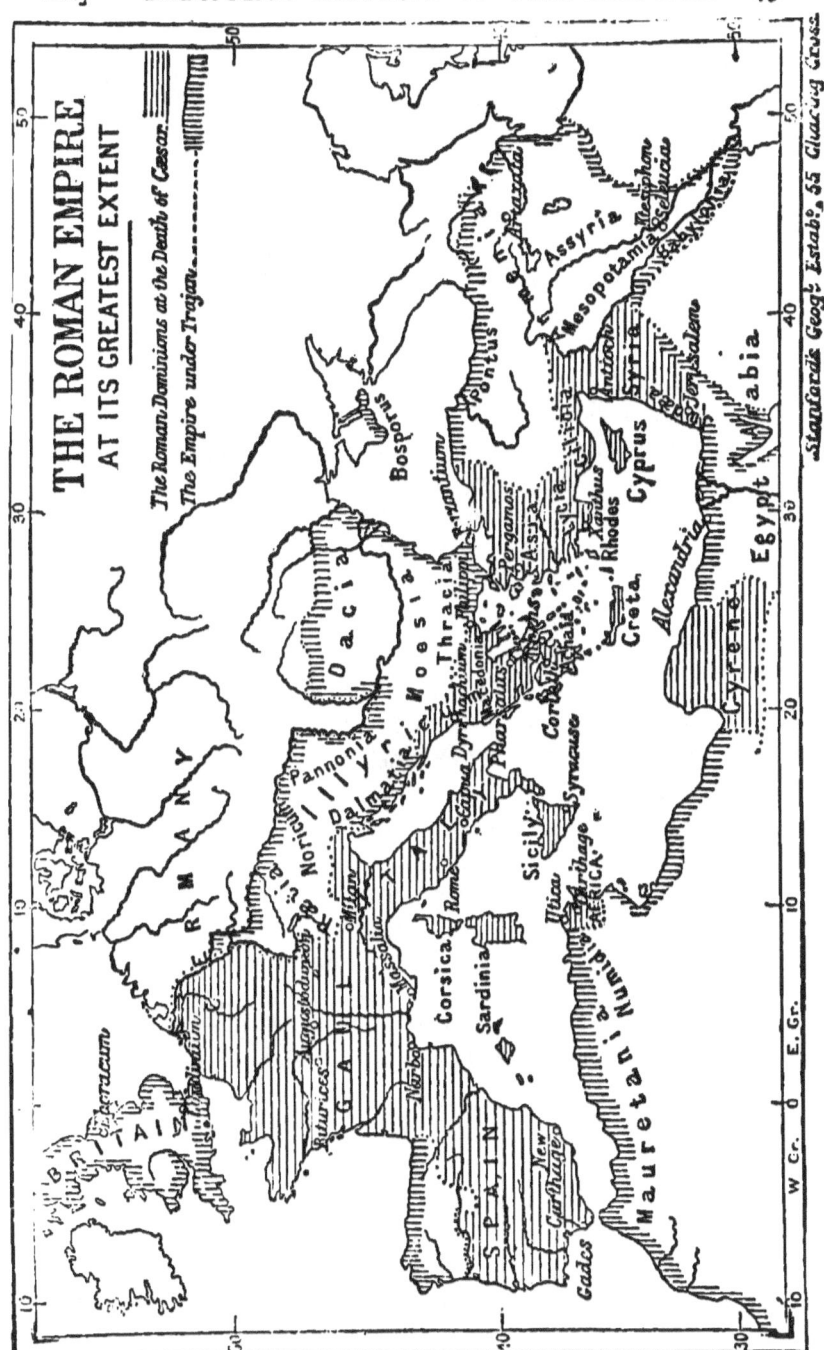

Marcus Aurelius. These formed an artificial family; each was succeeded, not by a real, but by an adopted son. All this time, the laws were observed and the senate was held in respect. It was now that the Empire reached its greatest extent. The **Dacians**, who lived north of the lower Danube, were subdued by Trajan, and their country was a province, the only great possession of Rome through the Danube. Trajan also had wars with the Parthians, and he added the provinces of Armenia, Mesopotamia, and Assyria, so that the Empire reached to the Caspian Sea. But this great dominion was only for a moment; for, as soon as Trajan was dead, his successor Hadrian, gave up all his eastern conquests. Thus under **Trajan** the Roman Empire was greater than it ever was before or after. Before long, Rome had to think more of defending what she had already got than of making any fresh conquests.

23. **Summary.**—Thus it was that Rome became the mistress of all that was then the civilized world. First, the settlements on the neighbouring hills were joined into one city. Then that city became the head, first of Latium and then of all Italy. Then all the lands round the Mediterranean became, first dependencies and then provinces, of Rome; and lastly, the inhabitants of those provinces became Roman citizens. Meanwhile, in the internal history, first came the kings, then the early commonwealth with the disputes between patricians and plebeians; step by step the plebeians won equal rights with the patricians; then came the struggle between the rich and the poor; and, lastly all power came into the hands of one man, and the state was in truth changed from a commonwealth into a monarchy. Everything at Rome, in war and in peace, was done step by step, and for this reason the power of Rome was much more lasting than any other. Not reckoning the momentary conquests of Trajan in the East, the Roman Empire at its greatest

extent took in all Europe within the Rhine and the Danube, together with the one province of Dacia beyond the Danube and the greater part of the Isle of Britain. In Asia it took in all the lands west of the Euphrates. In Africa it took in Egypt and the narrow slip of fertile land north of the Great Desert. It thus took in all the civilized part of the old world, all the old dominions and settlements of Phœnicia, Greece, and Macedonia. Rome was now the champion of the West against the East, and it was only in the far East that she had a rival on equal terms in the kingdom of Parthia.

CHAPTER IV.

THE DECLINE OF ROME.

1. **Wars with the Persians and Germans.**— The two chief enemies of Rome were now the Persians in the East, and the Germans in the West. After Trajan's time, the Parthian power grew up again; but in 226 the old **Persians** rose again and formed a national kingdom under Ardeshir or **Artaxerxes**, whose descendants were the **Sassanid** Kings of Persia. Rome and Persia were now rivals, often fighting along the frontier, but neither of them ever touching the real strength of the other. The warfare in the West was very different. From the time of Marcus Aurelius, the German nations began to threaten the Empire along the whole frontier of the Rhine and the Danube. This marks one of the great changes in the history of the world. Rome no longer advanced; she could only defend her frontiers against the people who were soon to take her place as the leading people of Europe. Our own forefathers were still in Germany, but they lived too far off to have anything to

do with what was now going on. The chief Teutonic nations with whom Rome had to strive were the **Franks** along the Rhine, and the **Goths** along the Danube. They pressed into the Empire in various ways, sometimes by warlike inroads, sometimes by serving in the Roman armies and being rewarded with lands. Sometimes again the Romans won great victories, drove back the Germans, and harried their lands. Still the Germans were rising and the Romans were sinking. Rome's day of conquest was past; she was now fighting only to keep what she had got.

2. **Emperors chosen by the Army.**—The last of the five good Emperors, Marcus Aurelius was succeeded by his own son Commodus. He was one of the worst Emperors, and was murdered in 192. Then came nearly a hundred years, up to 285, in which Emperors were set up and, often after a short time, killed by the soldiers. Sometimes two or more armies in different parts of the Empire each chose its own general, so that there were several Emperors reigning in different parts. But these rival Emperors did not found separate kingdoms. Each tried to get the whole Empire if he could; and commonly one in the end got the better of the others, and then those who failed were called **Tyrants**. For a little while something like a dynasty was kept up in the family of **Septimius Severus**, who reigned from 193 to 211. It was in the time of his son Antoninus or Caracalla that all the old distinctions were swept away, and all the free inhabitants of the empire became Romans. After this many of the Emperors were what before would have been called barbarians, especially many wise and brave men from Illyria, as Decius, Claudius, Aurelian, and above all Diocletian. But few of them reigned any long time, and once, in the days of Valerian and his son Gallienus, from 253 to 268, so many rival Emperors reigned at once that they were called the

Thirty Tyrants. With Diocletian, in 284, a new state of things begins.

3. **Diocletian and his Successors.**—By this time men had found out that the Roman state was no longer a commonwealth, and, now that the provincials had become Roman citizens, they found out that the Roman state was something more than the city of Rome. From Diocletian's time, the Emperors, though they still never took the title of King, took to themselves far more of kingly pomp; and, as they were so often wanted nearer the frontiers, other cities than Rome began to be their chief dwelling-places. Diocletian's plan was to have two head Emperors, called Augusti, and two Cæsars under them. The Empire was divided into four parts: Italy and the neighbouring lands, the Western, the Greek, and the Eastern provinces. Milan and Nikomêdeia in Asia were to be the capitals of the two Augusti, and Trier or York in the West, and Antioch in the East, those of the two Cæsars. But in 303 Diocletian abdicated, and long civil wars followed, till the whole Empire was united in 323 under **Constantine**, called the Great.

4. **The Growth of Christianity.**—Constantine was the first Emperor who declared himself a Christian. The Christian religion began about the same time as the Roman Empire, for our Lord Jesus Christ was born under the reign of Augustus and crucified under the reign of Tiberius. Since then the Christian religion, though often persecuted, had been gradually spreading. It may seem strange that the Christians were, as a rule, most persecuted, not under the worst Emperors, but under the best, such as Trajan, Marcus, Decius, and Diocletian himself. This was because the heathen religion of Rome was part of the constitution of the state, and those who refused to worship the gods of Rome were looked on as enemies of the **Emperor** and of the commonwealth. Hence those

Emperors who were most anxious to keep up the old laws of Rome were the hardest persecutors of the Christians. But the heathen religion had now become a mere affair of state, in which few men really believed, whilst the Christians believed with all their hearts in what they professed. Thus Christianity was the growing and paganism the sinking power; and, as soon as the Emperors became Christians, paganism began to die out.

5. **Constantine and his Family.**—The reign of Constantine is one of the great epochs in Roman history. It is marked by three great changes. Under him the Empire became, in form as well as in truth, a despotism resting on the army. The Senate and the Consuls were now mere shadows. Secondly, now that the Emperors had forsaken Rome, Constantine founded a new capital at the old Greek city of Byzantion on the Bosporos, to which he gave the name of **New Rome**, but which has ever since been called **Constantinople** or the city of Constantine. It was much more easy for him both to set up his despotic power, and to establish the Christian religion in this new city, than it could have been in the Old Rome. Thus, while in the Old Rome paganism died out very slowly, the New Rome was a Christian city from the beginning. Moreover, Constantine reigned longer than any Emperor since Augustus, and the Empire stayed in his family as long as there were any of them left. But most of them were cut off by their own kinsfolk. Constantine died in 337; then the Empire was divided among his three sons, but was joined again under Constantius in 350. In his time there were several rival Emperors, and there were unsuccessful wars with the Germans and Persians. But in 361 Constantius was succeeded by his cousin **Julian**, who had been Cæsar in Gaul, and had won back the land from the Germans. He now made an expedition against the Persians, in which he was killed in 363. He was the last of the

family of Constantine, and the first act of the next Emperor Jovian was to give up several provinces to Persia.

6. Christianity the Religion of the Empire.

—After the time of Constantine, Christianity spread itself over the whole Empire, and even those who were still pagans learned very much from its preaching. Such was the Emperor Julian, who had been brought up a Christian, but fell back into paganism, and did all he could to bring back the old worship. Yet Julian himself was, in his own life, one of the best of the Emperors. But nothing could now stop the growth of the new religion, and by the end of the century the public worship of paganism was forbidden. Christianity, in its birth an Asiatic and Semitic religion, had become the religion of the Roman Empire. And to this day Christianity is the religion of all those nations which either formed part of the Roman Empire, or have learned their religion and civilization from it. Outside these bounds Christianity has made very little way. But, as soon as the persecution stopped, the Christians began to dispute among themselves. Constantius and several Emperors in the fourth century followed the doctrines of **Arius**, a priest of Alexandria, which were condemned by a General Council of the Church, held at Nice or Nikaia in Bithynia, in Constantine's time. It was the Arian form of Christianity which was first adopted by most of the Teutonic nations. In fact, Christianity split into divisions answering to the great divisions of the Empire. In after times, the Greek and the Latin provinces split asunder into the Eastern and Western Churches, while in the further East men fell away into doctrines differing from either. And, as at the beginning the Teutonic nations accepted Christianity in what was called an heretical shape, so in after times there arose a Teutonic form of Christianity, differing from either the Latin, the Greek, or the Eastern.

E. Pr. D

7. **The Gothic Invasions.**—In the fourth century the Teutonic nations began really to make settlements within the Empire. Hitherto there had been constant wars along the frontiers; but, Rome was commonly able to win back what she lost. Thus Constantine and Julian had driven back the German invaders of Gaul, and so did **Valentinian**, who, with his brother Valens, began to reign in 364. But now the Teutonic nations were pressed upon by the Huns, a Turanian people from Asia, and so pushed on still faster. In 376 the **Goths** were allowed to cross the Danube and settle in the Empire. But, being ill-treated by the Romans, they took to arms, and Valens was killed in a battle at Hadrianople. Then the Goths marched hither and thither, and all that could be done was to get them to enter the Roman service, and to give their Kings some Roman title. Under **Theodosius** the Great, by whom the whole Empire was again united in 392, things got a little better; when he died in 395, the Empire was divided between his sons, Arcadius in the East, and Honorius in the West. Then came the worst time of all. Honorius lived chiefly in the strong fortress of Ravenna. In 410 the West-Goths, under **Alaric**, sacked Rome, but their next King Ataulf went into Spain, nominally as a Roman officer. This was really the beginning of a Gothic kingdom in Spain and Gaul, the first Teutonic kingdom within the Empire.

8. **End of the Empire in Italy.**—Both in the East and in the West, the Empire stayed in the family of Theodosius as long as any of them were left. But meanwhile several Tyrants or rival Emperors arose, and the Western provinces were lopped off one by one by them, while the Eastern Emperors had to keep on the strife with Persia. By the middle of the fifth century the Western Emperors had lost all real power out of Italy, and Emperors were set up and put down by the commanders of the barbarian mercenaries. At last in 476 this first line of Western Emperors

came to an end. **Odoacer**, the chief of the mercenaries, took the power into his own hands; but the way in which the change was made shows how the old ideas still stayed in men's minds. The Roman Senate voted that one Emperor was enough and that the Western Empire should be joined again to the Eastern. Then the Eastern Emperor Zeno, now sole Emperor, gave Odoacer a commission to rule Italy as Patrician. Presently, in 489, Zeno, wishing to get the East-Goths out of the East, gave their King **Theodoric** another commission, under which he overthrew Odoacer, and reigned in Italy from 493 to 526. He ruled well, and his power reached far beyond Italy. His dominion was really an independent and powerful kingdom; formally he was king only of his own Goths, and ruled Italy as the Emperor's lieutenant. Thus the Roman Empire still went on under Emperors who reigned in the New Rome, but who had no real power in the Old.

9. **Formation of the Teutonic Kingdoms.**—The commission given by the Emperors to Ataulf thus led to the beginning of the West-Gothic kingdom in Spain and Southern Gaul, and the like commission given to Theodoric led to the beginning of an East-Gothic kingdom in Italy and the neighbouring lands. Meanwhile Teutonic kingdoms were formed in other parts of the West. Thus the **Burgundians** founded a kingdom in South-eastern Gaul; and in 451 there was a fear that all Gaul and all Europe might fall under the power of the Hunnish king **Attila**. But he was happily overthrown at Châlons by the Roman general Aëtius and the West-Gothic King Theodoric, who must not be confounded with the great Theodoric. The Roman power in Gaul died out slowly, but all Northern Gaul came into the power of the **Franks** under their first Christian King **Chlodwig** or Clovis, who reigned from 481 to 511. The Franks now gradually gained the chief power both in Germany and in Gaul; but they settled only in a small part of

each country, part keeps the Frankish name still, being called, the one **Franken** or **Franconia**, and the other **France**. Before this, in 429, the **Vandals** passed through Spain and Africa, and founded a kingdom there. All these Teutonic nations were at first Arians, except only the Franks; for Chlodwig was baptized by a Catholic Bishop. It was out of the Frankish kingdom that the great kingdoms of Germany and France afterwards grew.

10. **The Teutonic and Romance Languages.**—The Teutonic settlers who founded kingdoms within the Empire were not mere destroyers. They were the disciples of the Romans as well as their conquerors. At first the Romans and Germans lived each according to their own law, under the rule of the German Kings. And, as the Germans were Christians, they respected the churches and clergy, and those who were Arians gradually came over to the Catholic faith. It was only under the Vandals in Africa that the Catholics suffered much from their Arian masters. And gradually in Gaul, Spain, and Italy, both Germans and Romans came to speak such Latin as was then spoken. This was not the Latin of books, but the common Latin of the people, into which a good many German words crept in. Thus arose several of the great languages of Europe, **Italian**, **Spanish**, **Provençal** in Southern, and **French** in Northern, Gaul. All these languages are Latin, more or less broken up and mixed with German words and idioms. But outside the Empire men still kept the old Teutonic tongues, called **Theotisc, Deutsch, or Dutch**, meaning the tongue of the people, the tongue that could be understood. The Romans and Celts, whose language they did not understand, they called **Welsh**, or strangers. Of this Teutonic or Dutch tongue there are two great divisions, the **High-Dutch**, spoken by the Franks and other inland German nations, and the

Low-Dutch, spoken by the Saxons and other nations nearer to the shores of the Ocean.

11. **The English Conquest of Britain.**— All these Teutonic conquests were made by land, for the crossing of the Vandals from Spain into Africa can hardly be called a conquest by sea. But the great conquest made by the Low-Dutch tribes was made by sea. This was our own conquest of Britain. Till the latter part of the fourth century our forefathers, the **Angles, Saxons,** and **Jutes,** stayed in their old homes in Northern Germany and had nothing to do with the Romans. But in the reign of Valentinian the Saxons attacked Britain by sea, but were driven off by Theodosius, the father of the Emperor of that name. As the Saxons were thus the first Low-Dutch people with whom the Celts of Britain had anything to do, they have always called all the Teutonic settlers **Saxons.** In 410 Honorius withdrew the Roman troops from Britain, and the provincials were left to themselves. So our forefathers soon began to settle in the land. First, in 449, the Jutes founded the kingdom of Kent; then came more Saxons, and then Angles. And, as the Angles took the greater part of the land, when all their tribes were one nation with a common name, they were called Angles or **English,** and their land **England.** Our forefathers, step by step, drove out or slew the Britons or **Welsh,** and, in about one hundred years after their first coming, they had won all the eastern part of the island, from the Isle of Wight to the Forth. But the Britons still stayed in the west, and the Picts and Scots in the north. The English conquest of Britain was very unlike the other Teutonic conquests; for the English had never learned to look up to Rome, or serve in her armies. So they destroyed everything Roman, and kept their Teutonic language and heathen worship. When they were afterwards converted, it

was not by the Welsh or Britons, but by a special mission from Rome.

12. **Summary.**—Thus, in the course of the fourth and fifth centuries, Christianity gradually became the religion of the Roman Empire, and from thence of the Teutonic nations who settled in the Empire by land. Out of these settlements by land, those of the Goths, Franks, and others, the Romance nations and languages of modern Europe arose. Meanwhile the English came into Britain by sea. By these conquests the Western Empire was cut short, and at last what was left of it, namely Italy, was nominally joined again to the Eastern. All this while the New Rome or Constantinople remained the capital of the whole Empire, when it was united, and of the eastern part, when it was divided.

CHAPTER V.

THE ROMAN EMPIRE IN THE EAST.

1. **The Roman Emperors at Constantinople.**—Thus there was no longer an Emperor anywhere in the West; but the Roman Empire still went on at **Constantinople.** The Emperors who now reigned there had no real power west of the Hadriatic. But they were ready, whenever they had a chance, to win back any of the lost provinces. Their dominion took in the Greek and the Eastern lands. Latin was still the official language, but Greek was now the common speech, and Constantinople was the chief seat of Greek learning. Thus no Teutonic kingdoms were formed within the Eastern Empire: there was much marching and settling of Teutonic, Slavonic, and even Turanian, nations on the northern

frontier, by whom the Empire was often threatened and invaded. At the beginning of this time there was peace with Persia, but presently the endless wars in these parts began again.

2. **The Recovery of Africa and Italy.**—The most famous Emperor of this time is **Justinian**, who reigned from 527 to 565. His greatest work at home was causing the laws of Rome to be put into a regular code called the **Civil Law**, which has been the groundwork of the law of most part of Europe ever since. And he was able to win back a large part of the lost dominion of the Empire. The Vandal kingdom in Africa had now greatly gone down, and in 534 **Belisarius** the great general of Justinian, won Africa back for the Empire. About the same time, the south of Spain was won back also. And, after the death of the great Theodoric, Justinian thought that Italy also might be won back from the East-Goths. And so it was, after a war which lasted from 535 to 553, first under Belisarius and then under **Narses**. Thus Justinian reigned over both the Old and the New Rome, and the Empire again stretched from the Ocean to the Euphrates, round the greater part of the Mediterranean. But this great power did not last long after Justinian's death. For in 568 the **Lombards**, a Teutonic people, passed into Italy: from them Northern Italy is still called **Lombardy**. From this time part of Italy was held by the Lombards, and part by the Emperors. The Emperors kept the three great islands and a part of Southern Italy; also Rome and Ravenna and the country about them, and the **Venetian Islands**, whither men had fled in the fifth century for fear of the Huns. These dominions were ruled by an **Exarch** or governor, who lived at Ravenna. Thus, as neither the Emperor nor his deputy lived at Rome, the Bishops gradually got the chief power there. They were called in a special way Popes, and their power over the whole Western Church greatly grew.

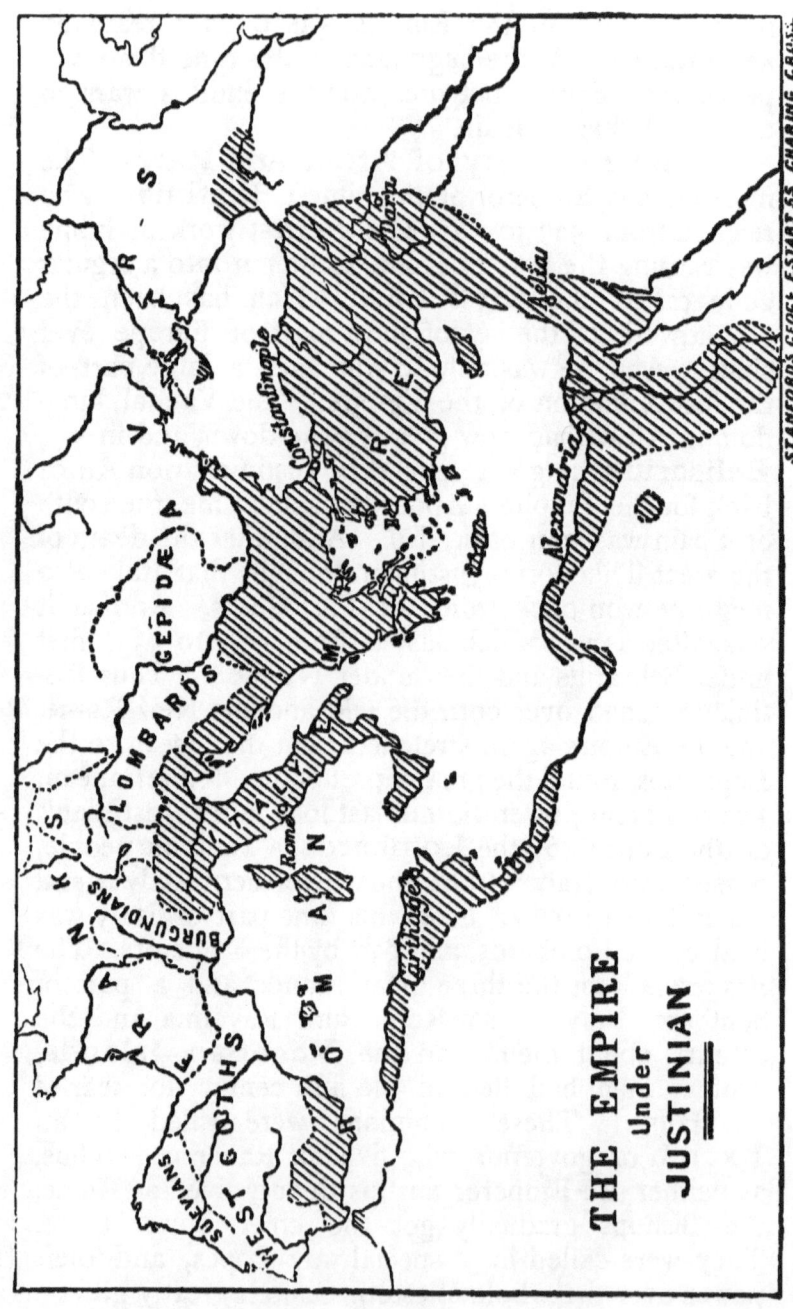

3. **Wars with Persia.**—While the Empire thus grew again under Justinian, the rival kingdom of **Persia** was also very powerful under its King **Chosroes** or **Nushirvan**, and under his grandson, another **Chosroes**, Persia reached the height of her power. Between the years 611 and 615 Chosroes overran all Egypt, Syria, and Asia. Presently the Emperor **Heraclius** crossed into Asia, and, in a great war from 620 to 625, altogether broke the Persian power and won back all that had been lost. But meanwhile the West-Goths won back the Roman province in Spain. And both Romans and Persians were so weakened by these long wars that neither of them had strength left to withstand an enemy whom none of them looked for, but which was altogether to change the face of the world both in Europe and Asia.

4. **The Rise of the Saracens.**—We now come to a time when, for the first time since the destruction of Carthage, a Semitic people play a chief part. The **Arabs** or **Saracens** were now formed into one nation and filled with religious zeal by the teaching of **Mahomet**. He was born in 569 at Mecca, the holy city of Arabia. He taught a new religion, the third of the three Semitic religions which have taught men that there is but one God. He said that both the Jewish and Christian religion had come from God, but that he was sent to teach a more perfect faith still. In his own country he was a reformer, for he taught the Arabs to forsake idolatry and to make themselves into one nation. By his law all men everywhere were to be given their choice of **Koran**, **Tribute**, or **Sword**; that is, that they were either to accept the teaching of his book called the **Koran**, to buy the right of practising their own religion by paying tribute, or else to fight against the Saracens. These terms have been offered to other nations by all Mahometan conquerors ever since. Mahomet himself died in 632, after he had brought all Arabia

under his own power, but before he had done much
to subdue other lands.

5. **Conquests of the Saracens from the
Empire.**—After Mahomet's death, the chiefs of the
Saracens were called **Caliphs**, that is **Successors**.
They held the chief power, both spiritual and temporal, as if among the Christians the same man had
been Pope and Emperor at once. The first three
Caliphs were **Abou-Bekr, Omar**, and **Othman**;
then came Mahomet's son-in-law **Ali**. But many held
that Ali ought to have succeeded at once, so that the
power might have stayed among the Prophet's own
children. There were great divisions about this afterwards; but at first all the Saracens obeyed Abou-Bekr
and Omar. They attacked the Roman and Persian
dominions at once, and between 632 and 639 the
Roman provinces of Syria and Egypt were lost to
Christendom. These were the lands which had never
really become either Greek or Roman,- and which
therefore easily fell away. But in the Greek lands
west of Mount Tauros the Saracens ravaged, but
never really conquered. Twice, in 673 and 716, they
besieged Constantinople, but both times they were
driven back. Of the Latin provinces, they invaded
Africa in 647, but they could not take Carthage till
698, and the whole country was not conquered till
709. Next, in 710, they crossed over into **Spain**,
overthrew the West-Gothic kingdom, and conquered
the whole land, save the mountains in the north,
where the Christians still held out. From Spain they
crossed into Gaul and conquered the province of
Narbonne or Septimania. This they held only for
a short time, but it took more than seven hundred
years wholly to drive them out of Spain.

6. **The Saracens in the East.**—While the
Saracens thus cut short the Roman Empire, they
altogether conquered **Persia**. Between 632 and 651,
they won the whole land; the old Persian religion

died out, and Persia gradually became a Mahometan country. But, just as Syria and Egypt had a form of Christianity of their own, so Persia made a form of Mahometanism of its own, the sect which specially reverences Ali. After Ali's murder in 660, the **Ommiad** Caliphs reigned at Damascus, the Saracens still went on conquering, and there was a moment when one man reigned from Spain to Sind. But in 755 this great dominion was divided. In 750 the Ommiad dynasty were overthrown by the **Abbassides**, the descendants of Mahomet's uncle Abbas, who moved their capital to Bagdad. But an Ommiad prince named Abd-al-Rahman escaped to Spain, and there founded a dynasty. Soon the **Turks** from beyond the Oxus began to press into the Saracen dominions, half as conquerors, half as disciples, just as the Teutons and Slaves pressed into the Eastern and Western Empires. And step by step the Saracenic dominion was cut up among Turkish dynasties, whose submission to the Caliph was merely nominal. This was nearly the same as what happened among the Christians; only, as the Caliph was both spiritual and temporal head, we may say that he went on being Pope after he had ceased to be Emperor.

7. **The Growth of the Franks.**—While the Saracens thus cut short the Empire in Asia and Africa, a power grew up which was to supplant the Emperors at Constantinople in the West. The **Franks**, were the chief people in Germany and Gaul. The **Merwings** or Kings of the House of Chlodwig had become weak and divided; but the Frankish power was renewed under the **Karlings**, who came from the Eastern or German part of the Frankish dominions, and ruled, first in the name of the Merowingian Kings as **Mayors of the Palace**, and afterwards as Kings themselves. The most famous of these mayors was **Karl** or **Charles**, surnamed **Martel**, or the Hammer. In his time the Saracens tried to enlarge

their dominion in Gaul, but they were overthrown by Charles in the **Battle of Tours** in 732, and in 755 they were driven out of Gaul altogether. But long after this they made inroads both by sea and land into both Gaul and Italy. The Karlings became kings in 753 when the last Merwing Chilperic was deposed and **Pippin**, the son of Charles Martel, was chosen King. After Pippin came his son **Charles the Great**, who began to reign in 768. Under him the Frankish power extended every way. He had stronger power over Southern Germany and Gaul, and he conquered the **Saxons**, that is the Old-Saxons who had stayed in Germany and had not come into Britain, and who were still heathens. Thus the Franks became the ruling people of all Germany. Charles had also wars with the Danes to the North, and with the Slaves and other nations to the East of Germany, and he added Spain as far as the Ebro to the Frankish dominion. And he presently won a still higher place for himself and his nation.

8. **The new Empire of the West.**—All through the seventh century the Emperors kept their hold on Rome, Ravenna, and the rest of their lands in Italy. But in the eighth century, the greater part of this dominion slipped away. In 718, after a time of great confusion, the Empire came to **Leo the Isaurian**, who beat back the Saracens in their second siege of Constantinople, and so saved Christendom in the East, as Charles Martel soon after did in the West. In 741 came his son Constantine, who also fought bravely against the Saracens. But while Leo and Constantine thus strengthened the Empire at one end, they weakened it at the other. A dispute now arose about the reverence paid to images or pictures in churches. This the Emperors and many men in the East thought idolatrous, and were called **Iconoclasts** or image-breakers. But in Italy men clave to their images, and the Bishops

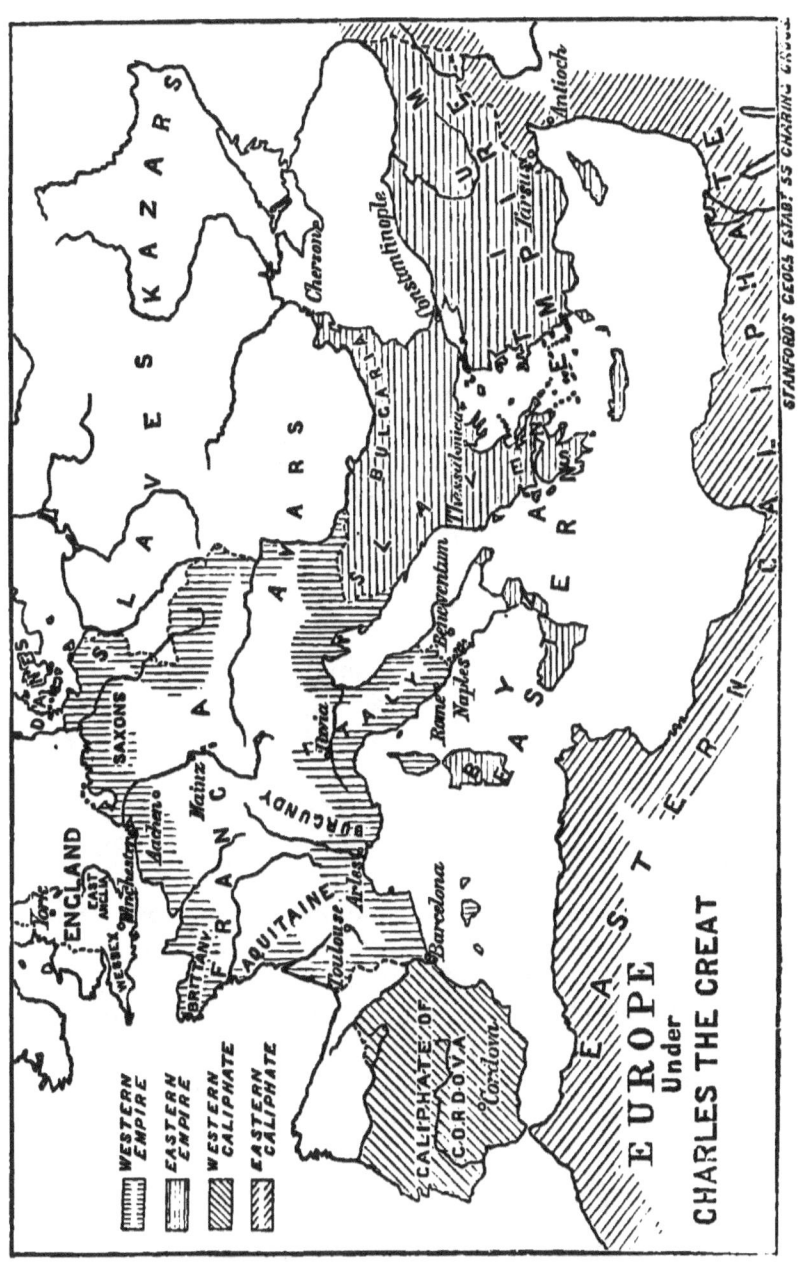

of Rome, the second and third Gregories, strongly withstood the Iconoclast Emperors. Thus the Imperial power in Rome grew weaker, while the Lombards pressed on, took Ravenna, and threatened Rome. Then the Romans and their Bishops called in the Franks to help them. So Pippin came, won back Ravenna, saved Rome, and ruled as **Patrician**, for men still shrank from quite throwing off the authority of the Emperor. Then in 774 Pippin's son, Charles the Great, overthrew the Lombard kingdom, and was thus master of all Italy, except the South. But the authority of the Emperors at Constantinople was not formally thrown off till the year 800. Eirênê, the mother of Constantine the Sixth, the last of the Isaurians, had deposed and blinded her son and reigned in his stead. But in the West men said that a woman could not be Cæsar and Augustus, and that the Old Rome had a better right than the New to choose the Roman Emperor. So the Romans would not acknowledge Eirênê, but chose their Patrician Charles to be Emperor, and he was crowned by Pope Leo and called **Charles Augustus**.

9. **The two Empires and the two Caliphates.** —Thus there was again a separate Western Empire and the Emperors of the East and of the West each claimed to be the only true Emperor. Besides their dominion beyond the Hadriatic, the Eastern Emperors still kept Sicily and part of Southern Italy. The Western Empire, under Charles the Great, took in the rest of Italy, with Germany, Gaul, and part of Spain. And now each Empire begins to be attached to a particular nation. The Western Empire now becomes German, and the Eastern Empire becomes Greek; for the dominions of the Eastern Emperors now answer nearly to those parts of Europe and Asia where Greek was the chief language. In these lands Greek was the one language for all purposes, while in the West

men mostly spoke German and wrote Latin. Moreover, the division of Christendom between the Eastern and Western Empire answers to the division of the Mahometan power. The Ommiad princes in Spain after a while called themselves Caliphs, so that there was an Eastern and a Western Caliphate. These four were the chief states of the civilized world. Now we might have looked to see all Christians united on one side and all Mahometans on the other. But, owing to their divisions, each of the four powers was an enemy to the more distant power of the other religion, and a friend of the nearer one. The Eastern Empire was at war with the Eastern Caliphate, but was commonly on good terms with the Western. And so Charles the Great had wars with the Saracens in Spain, but he was on good terms with the Caliph of Bagdad. Beyond the two Empires and the two Caliphates lay the nations who were still only growing up, as the English and Scandinavians in Western Europe, the Slaves and others in Eastern Europe, and the Turks far away in Asia.

10. **Summary.**—Thus, at the end of the fifth century, the Western Empire was nominally reunited to the Eastern, while in truth the West was cut up into Teutonic kingdoms. In the sixth century the Emperors who reigned at Constantinople won back much of their lost dominion, all Italy and Africa and part of Spain. But soon a great part of Italy was again conquered by the Lombards. In the seventh century Persia first threatened to destroy Rome, and then Rome to destroy Persia. Then the Saracens overwhelmed Persia altogether, lopped off the Eastern and African provinces of Rome, and won nearly all Spain and a small part of Gaul. Meanwhile the Franks united all Germany and Gaul under their power. They were then called into Italy, and their King was chosen to be Emperor by the Old Rome, in opposition to the New. Thus in the ninth century there were again two Roman

Empires; but now they had become quite separate states, and one was German and the other Greek. In like manner the Mahometan power had been broken into two Caliphates, and the Turks were pressing on into the Eastern one.

CHAPTER VI.

THE FOUNDATION OF THE EUROPEAN NATIONS.

1. **The Frankish Empire and its Divisions.** —Thus a German King became Roman Emperor of the West, and ruled over many lands over which the earlier Emperors had not ruled. All Africa and most part of Spain had been cut away; part of Italy belonged to the other Empire; but all Germany was now part of the Western Empire. But an Emperor who was a German King was very unlike an Emperor who reigned at Rome or at Constantinople. And only a man like Charles the Great could keep so great a dominion together. After the reign of his son **Lewis the Pious**, from 814 to 839, the great Frankish Empire was divided among Charles's grandsons. One was to be Emperor, and the others to be Kings under him. But they were always quarrelling and seizing each other's kingdoms. At last, in 884, nearly all the Empire of Charles the Great was joined together under **Charles the Fat.** But in 887 all his kingdoms deposed him, and chose separate Kings. Out of this division of the Empire the chief continental states of Western Europe gradually arose. At first there were four kingdoms; that of the **East-Franks**, which grew into the kingdom of **Germany**; that of the **West-Franks**, which grew into the kingdom of **France**, and the kingdoms of **Italy** and **Burgundy**.

2. **The Western Kingdom or France.**—Till the ninth century there was nothing at all like the modern kingdom of **France**. But in the division of the Empire among the sons of Lewis, his son **Charles the Bald** got a kingdom which was something like it, though it did not stretch nearly so far to the East. This was the kingdom of the West-Franks, which was called, from Charles's own name, **Karolingia**. So the lands on the Rhine, between the Eastern and Western kingdoms, which had been ruled by two Kings called Lothar, were called **Lotharingia**, and part of that land is still called **Lothringen** or **Lorraine**. By the end of the ninth century, the dukes and counts in the Western kingdom had grown into princes who paid the King only nominal homage. The greatest of these were the Dukes of **Western Francia**, whose capital was Paris, and who were called **Dukes of the French**. At the division in 887 **Odo** of Paris was chosen King of the West-Franks; and from 887 to 987 the kingdom was sometimes held by a Duke of the French at **Paris**, sometimes by a Karling reigning at **Laon**. But the lands south of the Loire took very little heed to either of them. At last, in 987, **Hugh Capet**, Duke of the French, was chosen King, and the crown stayed in his family for eight hundred years. Thus the Duke of the French became King of the West-Franks. Thus too Paris became the capital of the kingdom. And, as the Kings at Paris got hold of the lands of their vassals and neighbours, the name of **Karolingia** was forgotten, and the name of their duchy of **France** was spread over most part of Gaul.

3. **The Kingdom of Burgundy.**—The name of **Burgundy** has many meanings, but as yet it always meant some part of the old **Burgundian** land in South-Eastern Gaul. Among the divisions of the ninth century, a Burgundian kingdom arose in

E. Pr.　　　　　　　　　　　　　　　　　E

the lands between the Rhône, the Saône, and the Alps, taking in the lands of Provence, Savoy, Bresse, Wallis, and others, and many famous cities, as Marseilles, Lyons, Vienne, Geneva, and **Arles**, from which the kingdom was sometimes called the kingdom of Arles. This Burgundian kingdom lasted, sometimes under one King, sometimes under two, till 1032, when Burgundy ceased to be a separate kingdom and henceforth had the same Kings as Germany.

4. **The Kingdom of Italy.**—In the division of the Empire, **Italy** was to be the special kingdom of the Emperor. Several Kings of Italy were crowned Emperors, but after 887 they had no power out of Italy, and not much in it. The land was often plundered by the Saracens, and, in the latter part of the ninth century, the dominions of the Eastern Emperors in Southern Italy were greatly enlarged. After 962 Italy had the same Kings as Germany.

5. **The Eastern Kingdom or Germany.**—The head kingdom meanwhile was the kingdom of the Eastern Franks, which grew into the kingdom of Germany. Here the Karlings reigned till 887, and for two reigns after. The first King of the East-Franks after the division was **Arnulf.** King Odo of Paris became his man, and he was afterwards crowned Emperor at Rome. After Arnulf's son Lewis, came Conrad, the first King who was not a Karling, and the crown came to the **Saxon** Kings. The first of them was **Henry,** who was chosen in 918; then came his son **Otto** the Great from 936 to 972, then Otto the Second and Third; and lastly Henry the Second, in whom the Saxon line ended in 1024. The border land of Lotharingia for a while fluctuated between the Eastern and Western kingdom; but from 987, when the Dukes of Paris became Kings, Lotharingia became an undoubted part of Germany. The Eastern Kings had also wars with the Danes to the North, and with the Slavonic nations to the

North-east, the Wends, Poles, and Bohemians. But their worst enemies were to the South-east, where a Turanian people, the **Magyars** or Hungarians, made many inroads into Germany and Italy. King Henry had much fighting with them, and they were at last driven out by Otto the Great in 954. The Eastern kingdom was the central state of Europe, and had to do with all parts of the world.

6. The Restoration of the Empire.—Up to this time there had been no regular succession in the Empire. Kings of different kingdoms had been Emperors; and since 887 there was often no generally acknowledged Emperor at all. But now that Germany was the greatest of the Frankish kingdoms, the German Kings joined both the kingdom of Italy and the Roman Empire to their own kingdom. In 951 Otto the Great was asked to come into Italy, and the King Berengar became his man. In 962 he was again asked by Pope John the Twelfth and the Italians generally to put down Berengar altogether. This he did, and in 963 he was crowned Emperor at Rome. From this time it was held that whoever was chosen King in Germany had a right to be crowned King of Italy at Milan, and to be crowned Emperor at Rome. Commonly the Emperors lived in Germany, but they often came into Italy, and Otto the Third had schemes for making Rome again the real head of the world. Now that the German Kings were Emperors of the Rômans, they left off calling themselves Kings of the Franks; so the title of **Rex Francorum** stuck specially to the Kings of the West-Franks. But the Eastern **Francia, Franken** or **Franconia**, kept its name, and was a chief duchy of the German kingdom.

7. The Growth of the Kingdom of England. —Meanwhile most of the European nations begin to grow into something like their present shape.

Thus it was with Germany, France, and Italy, and with other nations both in the North and in the East of Europe. Among these, the Teutonic tribes that had settled in Britain gradually grew into the one kingdom of **England**. In 597 the conversion of the English to Christianity began by the preaching of **Augustine**, who was sent by Pope Gregory the Great, and was the first Archbishop of Canterbury. In less than a hundred years all the English became Christians, through the teaching, partly of the Romans, partly of the Scots. During the sixth and seventh centuries there was much striving for the mastery among the English kingdoms, chiefly among the three greatest, those of the **Northumbrians** in the North, of the **Mercians** in the middle, and of the **West-Saxons** in the South-west. But between 802 and 837 **Ecgberht** King of the West-Saxons brought all the English kingdoms and part of the Welsh under his power. The other kingdoms for a while kept their kings; but from this time the West-Saxon King was the head, like the Emperor on the mainland. Then in the latter half of the ninth century the Danes began to invade England, and many of them settled in the eastern part. But Wessex was saved from them by our famous King **Alfred**. Then in the tenth century the West-Saxon Kings grew powerful again. Step by step they overcame the Danes; they joined all England to their own kingdom, and won a supremacy over all Britain. Thus England became one kingdom. But towards the end of the tenth century the Danes came again, to conquer England as a whole kingdom, and to set a Danish king on the throne. This they at last did in 1016, when the Danish King **Cnut** became King of all England.

8. **The Scandinavian Nations.**—We have already spoken once or twice of the Danes, for the Teutonic nations of the north of Europe, the nations of the two peninsulas between the Ocean and

the Baltic, now began to play a great part. In the northern peninsula they were the first Aryan settlers, and they slew or drove out the Fins and Laps, of whom some remain both on the extreme north and on the eastern side of the Baltic. In the course of the eighth and ninth centuries they settled down into the three kingdoms of Denmark, Sweden and Norway. Of these, the Swedes pressed northward and eastward, against the Fins and into Russia, while the Danes had much to do both with the Empire and with England. And both the Danes and the Northmen or people of Norway plundered and settled in many lands. They made conquests in Ireland and Gaul, and settled in the far off lands of Iceland and Greenland. Early in the eleventh century the Scandinavian nations were at the height of their power; for Cnut reigned over England, Denmark, Norway, and part of Sweden. He had made a kind of Northern Empire to match those of the West and East; but, when he died in 1035, his great dominion was broken up.

9. **Foundation of the Duchy of Normandy.** —One settlement of the Northmen must be more specially mentioned. In the ninth century they plundered the coasts of Gaul, made some small settlements and more than once besieged Paris, At last, in 913, one of their chiefs, **Rolf**, called in Latin Rollo, made a greater settlement of which Rouen was the head. Charles the Simple, of the house of the Karlings, was then King of the West-Franks, and he and Robert, Duke of the French, agreed to give to Rolf part of the Duchy of France, all the land between the Seine and the Epte, if he would become a Christian, and hold his new lands in fief of the King. This, Rolf did, and both he and his successors greatly extended their dominion. As they learned to speak French, their name of Northmen was softened into **Normans**, and their land was called the Duchy of **Normandy**. The Dukes of the

Normans were mostly brave and wise princes, and their land became one of the chief states of Gaul and of Europe. They commanded the great river Seine, so that the Dukes and Kings of the French at Paris were quite cut off from the sea.

10. **The Eastern Empire and the Saracens.** —While nations were in this way forming in the West, they were forming in the East also. The Eastern Empire itself had in some sort become a nation, now that it so nearly answered to the Greek-speaking parts of Europe and Asia. And it was now beginning to be further cut off from western Europe by difference in religion. The Iconoclast controversy ended under Eirênê, at the end of the ninth century, in favour of the worshippers of images. But by this time other disputes had begun between the Eastern and Western Churches, chiefly because the Eastern Church would not submit to the growing claims of the Bishops of the Old Rome. Meanwhile Emperors of various dynasties reigned, under some of whom the Empire went down, while under others it rose again. In the course of the ninth century, the islands of Sicily and Crete were lost, and became the seat of Saracen powers. But, from the end of the ninth century till the beginning of the eleventh, under the Emperors of the Macedonian dynasty, the power of the Eastern Empire was again greatly increased. The Byzantine dominion in Italy was greatly extended; in 960 the Emperor **Nikêphoros Phokas** won back Crete, and in his reign, and in those of **John Tzimiskês** and **Basil the Second**, other great conquests were made. The Saracens were now split up into various small states, so that the Emperors were able to win back Antioch and other places which had been lost ever since the first Saracen conquests. The Roman frontier now again reached to the Euphrates.

11. **The Slavonic Nations.**—The Slavonic

nations now first begin to be of much importance. They form two great divisions, which had to do with the Eastern and the Western Empires severally. Those who lay to the north-west, bordering on Germany, got their Christianity from the Western Church, and became more or less connected with the German kingdom. Such were the **Wends** on the Baltic, the **Poles**, and the **Bohemians**. The Poles became Christians towards the end of the tenth century, and their Dukes and Kings gradually became independent of the Empire. But the Slaves in the South and East had most to do with the Eastern Empire, and they got their Christianity from the Eastern Church. The greatest of these Slavonic nations were the **Russians**, between whom and the Western Slaves lay the heathen **Prussians** and **Lithuanians**. To the south of the Poles lay Turanian nations, chiefly the Hungarians, who, after their defeat by Otto the Great, had settled down about the same time as the Poles. To the south of these were various Slavonic nations which had pressed into the Eastern Empire ever since the sixth century. The **Bulgarians** too, a Turanian people, were so mixed up with their Slavonic neighbours and subjects that they must count as Slavonic. With the Bulgarians and Russians the Emperors of the ninth and tenth centuries had much fighting. The Russians, who were under Scandinavian princes, had fleets on the Euxine, and more than once attacked Constantinople by sea. But they were defeated by John Tzimiskês, and soon after they became Christians of the Eastern Church. The Bulgarians, who had founded a kingdom in Macedonia and North-Western Greece, were at last subdued by Basil the Second. The Eastern Empire had now again won the frontier of the Danube, and it was more powerful than it had ever been since the reign of Heraclius. But when Basil was dead, it began to go down again.

12. **Summary.**—Thus, in the course of the ninth and tenth centuries, came the beginnings of the chief European nations. In the West, the kingdom of the **Franks**, which had been joined with the Western Empire under Charles the Great, split up into the four kingdoms of **Germany, France, Italy,** and **Burgundy.** Of these, the Western Empire was, under Otto the Great, joined to the kingdom of Germany, as also was the kingdom of Italy, and, after a while, that of Burgundy. In Gaul, the union of the Duchy of France with the Western kingdom led to the growth of the modern kingdom of **France.** In Britain, the kingdom of **England** was formed by the West-Saxon Kings joining together all the English kingdoms, and getting a lordship over the Scots and Welsh. In Scandinavia, the three kingdoms of **Denmark, Sweden,** and **Norway** were formed, and Scandinavian settlements are made in Britain, Gaul, and elsewhere, the chief of which grew into the Duchy of **Normandy.** For a moment, under **Cnut,** England and the greater part of Scandinavia were joined into a great Northern Empire. In the East, the **Eastern Empire** was becoming almost wholly Greek, and in the tenth century its power greatly revived, and many lands were won back from the Saracens in Asia and the Bulgarians in Europe. Meanwhile many of the Slavonic nations, especially the **Poles** and **Russians,** together with their Turanian neighbours the Hungarians, settled down into Christian kingdoms. In short, in the eleventh century, all Europe became Christian, except the Saracens in Spain and Sicily, the Prussians and Lithuanians, and the Fins and Laps quite in the North.

CHAPTER VII.

THE AGE OF THE CRUSADES.

1. **The Popes and the Emperors.**—We have now reached the times which are called the **Middle Ages**. We have left the old Roman times behind, and we have not yet come near to our own day. In Western Europe, the Teutonic settlements in the Roman provinces had formed new nations, new languages, and a new state of things. The Roman world had been changed both by Christian and by Teutonic ideas. In the West men held that the Roman Emperor was lord of the world; but the Roman Emperor was now a German King, and the Bishop of Rome had become a power alongside of the Emperor. Men still thought that Rome must be the spiritual and temporal head of the world. They held that God had two **Vicars** on earth, the **Emperor** in temporal things, and the **Pope** in spiritual things. But the Eastern Empire, and the Christians under the Eastern Caliphs, never acknowledged either of them. And even in the West, Britain and Scandinavia never formed part of the Empire, and Gaul and Spain fell away from it. Still men believed that the Emperor and the Pope were the two rightful chiefs of Christendom; only unluckily a great part of our history is made up of the quarrels between these two chiefs. As the power of the Emperors grew weaker, that of the Popes grew stronger. But whether the Pope or the Emperor got the better, it was still Rome that ruled.

2. **The Feudal Tenures.**—Meanwhile new doctrines grew up about the holding of land. The Roman Emperors had often granted lands on the frontier on the condition that their holders should do service in the wars. And the Teutonic Kings and

chiefs had a following of companions, who fought for them and whom they rewarded with lands. The chief was the **Lord**, and his followers were his **men**. Now when this Roman custom of holding lands by military service, and this Teutonic custom of personal faith to a lord, were joined together, a new state of things began. The man held his lands from his lord as a **fee** or **fief**, for which he owed service in war. This way of holding lands is called **feudal**. There was nothing like this in older times, for then it was held that a freeman's duty was to the state or to its chief, and not to any one man. But now men ceased to think much of the state or its chief; the King became the head lord in his kingdom, and not much more. Thus the kingdoms of Western Europe gradually broke up. The Dukes and Counts who held of the King grew into princes, paying their lord a mere nominal homage. This happened both in the Empire and in France. But in France the kings won the dominions of their vassals bit by bit, and so became masters of the whole land. In Germany the princes grew more and more independent, till the Empire became a mere name. In Italy the cities grew into independent commonwealths, as they did also to some extent in Germany and Burgundy. And men came to look on kingship as a property rather than an office; so most kingdoms became more strictly hereditary. The Empire was always elective, but France became more strictly hereditary than any other kingdom.

3. **The State of the Church.**—The state of the Church and of religion naturally differed greatly in the East, in the West, and in the lands under the Saracens. In these last the Christians were mere subjects, buying the right to practice their religion by the payment of tribute. They were often much oppressed, but not nearly so much while the Saracens ruled as afterwards when the Turks came. In the

Eastern Empire the Emperors never lost their power over the Church; and, wherever Greek was spoken, learning lived on among laymen as well as clergy. But in the West, especially after the time of the Karlings, learning quite died out among the laity; very few of them could even write, so that much temporal power came into the hands of the clergy, because they were fitter than other men for public business. The Bishops, Abbots, and other chief clergy had great estates and temporal powers, and held all kinds of temporal offices. In Germany the Prelates grew into princes like the Dukes and Counts, and everywhere they were chief members of the national assembly. Besides all this, the Popes tried to keep the clergy apart from other men, by forbidding them to marry, and forbidding them to be tried in any temporal court. They also said that no temporal lord might invest any clergyman with the symbols of his office. Out of this great disputes arose between the Popes and the Emperors. But in the East the parish clergy were always married, and the Emperors appointed and deposed the Patriarchs as they would.

4. **The Franconian Emperors.** — After the Saxon Emperors came the **Frankish** or **Franconian** Emperors, so called from the Eastern **Francia**. Under **Conrad**, the first Emperor of this house, Burgundy was joined to Germany and Italy in 1032. Then the great Emperor **Henry the Third** reigned from 1039 to 1056. He restored the royal power both in Germany and in Italy, and, turning out the bad Italian Popes who were disputing for the Popedom, appointed good German Bishops in their stead. His son **Henry the Fourth** was a child when he came to the kingdom. The Saxons revolted against him, and he had great strife with the famous **Hildebrand** or Pope **Gregory the Seventh** about the King's right to invest Bishops. Gregory took on him to depose the King, and set up enemies against him.

But in 1085 Henry drove Gregory out of Rome, and made a Pope of his own, Clement the Third, by whom he was crowned Emperor. Among Henry's enemies were his own sons, and when he died in 1106, he was at war with his son **Henry the Fifth**, who was afterwards Emperor. The Popes had set him up against his father; but, when his father was dead, he did much the same by them as his father had done.

5. **The Swabian Emperors.**—The next Emperor was Lothar of Saxony, who yielded much to the Popes. Then in 1138 came the great House of **Swabia** or **Hohenstaufen**. The first Swabian King, Conrad the Third, never was Emperor. In his day arose the names of **Welf** and **Waibling**, in Italy called **Guelf** and **Ghibelin**. The Ghibelins followed the Emperor; the Guelfs, called after **Welf** of Saxony who had rebelled against King Conrad, followed the Pope. Next came the great Emperor **Frederick**, called **Barbarossa** or the Red-beard, who reigned from 1152 to 1190. In Germany he had much strife with Duke Henry of Saxony, called the Lion, and the great Duchy of Saxony was broken up. But he is most famous for his strife with Pope Alexander the Third and the cities of Italy. These were now nearly independent, and made war and ruled over one another, like the cities of old Greece. The weaker cities called on the King to help them against Milan, and the strife went on till 1183, when the rights of the cities were acknowledged by the Peace of Constanz. Then came Henry the Sixth, and then, after a time of confusion, his son, **Frederick the Second**, called the Wonder of the World. He was crowned Emperor in 1220 and reigned till 1250. He had long strifes with the Guelfic cities and with one Pope after another. In 1245 Innocent the Fourth professed to depose him in a Council at Lyons; and in Germany he had to grant new privileges to the princes, so that the Imperial power was much weak-

ened in both kingdoms. Burgundy was now slipping away from the Empire altogether. With Frederick the Second the greatness of the Western Empire came to an end. His son Conrad succeeded, but he never was Emperor, and after him came a time of confusion from which the Empire never recovered

6. **England and France.**—Meanwhile England and France had much to do with each other. After Cnut and his sons, the English chose Edward the Confessor, one of the kingly house, who had spent his youth in Normandy. On his death in 1066, as there was no one in the kingly house fit to reign, they chose Earl **Harold**, who was the greatest man in the land. But **William** Duke of the Normans, called **William the Conqueror**, said that his kinsman King Edward had left him the crown. So he came over to England, King Harold was killed in the fight of Senlac or Hastings, and William was chosen King. Thus the same man was King of the English and Duke of the Normans. And, as there were always strifes between France and Normandy, so, now that Normandy and England had one prince, these grew into strifes between France and England. William the Conqueror, and his sons William Rufus and Henry the First, had wars with the French Kings Philip the First and Lewis the Sixth. Then, in 1154 the crown of England passed to **Henry the Second** of Anjou, who had married Eleanor, the heiress of Aquitaine. Thus one man ruled from Scotland to the Pyrenees, and the King of the English was far more powerful in Gaul than his lord the King of the French. But in 1204, **Philip Augustus** of France won Normandy and Anjou from King John of England, and the Kings of England kept nothing in Gaul but Aquitaine. And soon France grew to the south by winning the county of Toulouse, so that **Saint Lewis**, who reigned in France from 1226 to 1270, was master of

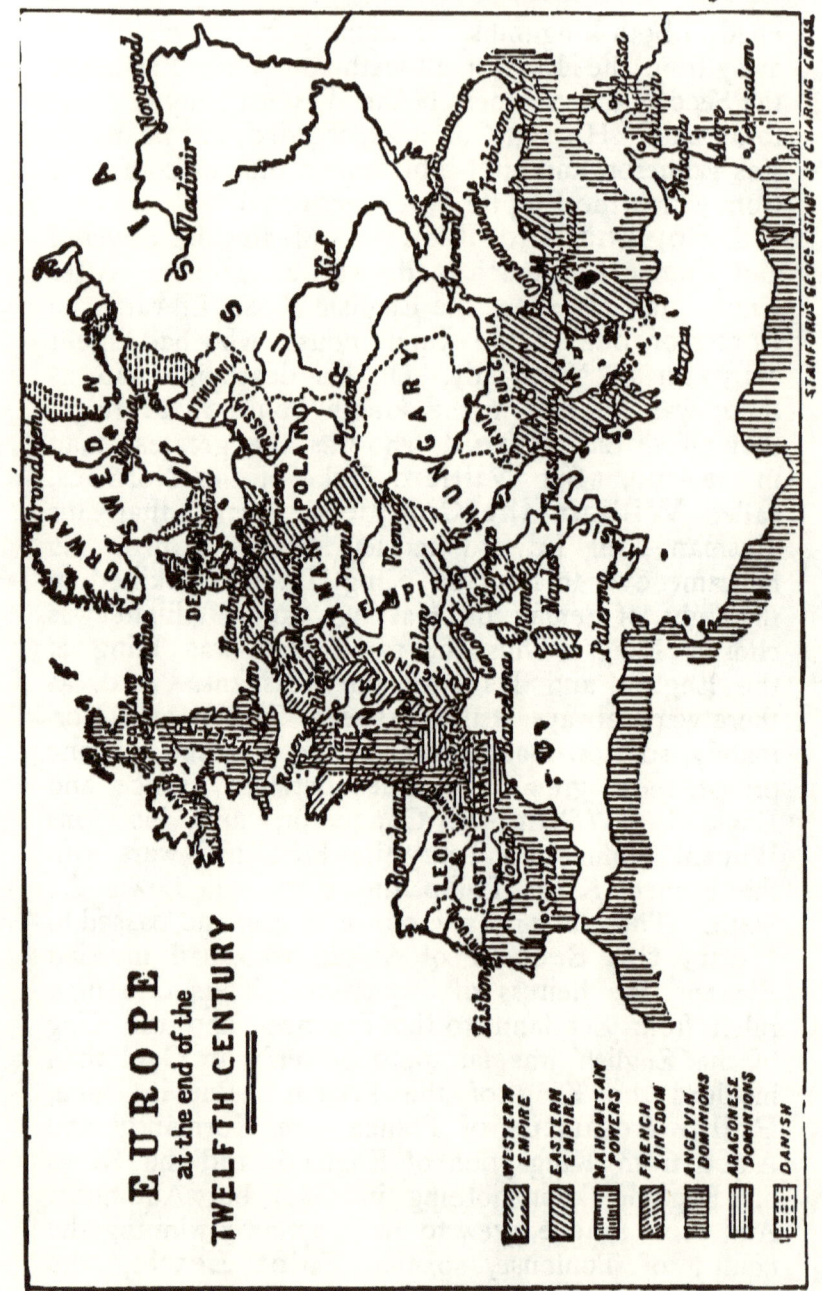

EUROPE at the end of the TWELFTH CENTURY

the more part of Gaul, and his dominion reached to the Channel, the Ocean, and the Mediterranean. And, as his brother Charles became Count of Provence, the French Kings began to get power in the kingdom of Burgundy.

7. **Advance of the Christians in Spain.**—All this time Christians and Mahometans were fighting wherever they met. The Christians now at last got the better of the Mahometans in Spain. The Spanish Caliphate was at the height of its power under **Abd-al-rahman** the Third from 912 to 961. But in 1031 it was cut up into several small kingdoms, and the Christians began to win back the land. In 1084 Alfonso the Sixth of **Leon** and **Castile** won the old capital of Toledo, and the Saracens in Spain called over the Moors from Africa to help them, which checked the Christians all during the twelfth century. But in the beginning of the thirteenth, the Christians again had the upper hand, and **Ferdinand the Third**, called **Saint Ferdinand**, who reigned from 1217 to 1252, won back **Seville** and **Cordova**. Meanwhile **Portugal** advanced on the West, and **Aragon** on the East; this last state had most to do with the general affairs of Europe. Its kings had large possessions in southern Gaul, but these they lost early in the thirteenth century. Thus the three main Spanish kingdoms, Castile, Aragon, and Portugal, all advanced, and from 1237, the Mahometans had only the one kingdom of **Granada**.

8. **The Kingdom of Sicily.**—While in Spain the Christian people of the land thus gained ground on the Saracens, foreign adventurers did the like in **Sicily**. All through the eleventh century parties of Normans came into Southern Italy, and under **Robert Wiscard** they won nearly all that the Eastern Emperors still kept. Thence, in 1062, they crossed into Sicily, and won the land from the Saracens. In 1130 Sicily became a kingdom, under King **Roger,** who

presently won all the places that either the other Normans or the Eastern Emperors kept in Italy, among them the city of Naples. The Kings of Sicily helped the Popes against the Emperor Frederick; but, on his death, Henry the Sixth claimed Sicily through his wife, and won it. Then came his son Frederick, who was afterwards the Emperor Frederick the Second; under him Sicily flourished greatly. When the Normans came into Sicily, the people were partly Christians speaking Greek, partly Mahometans speaking Arabic, while the Normans themselves spoke French. But from the time of Frederick Italian became the chief language, and the other tongues died out.

9. **The Eastern Empire and the Beginning of the Crusades.**—But the chief wars between Christians and Mahometans were in the East. After Basil the Second, the Eastern Empire went down again, and was soon cut short by the **Turks** in Asia. The Caliphs of Bagdad now lost all real power. A third set of Caliphs in Egypt gave out that they were descended from Fatima, Mahomet's daughter, which none of the other Caliphs were. Meanwhile various Turkish dynasties grew up in Asia, and in 1055 began the power of the **Seljuk** Sultans, who ruled over the whole East, and conquered all the Roman provinces in Asia. In 1092, they founded a kingdom at Nikaia, and called themselves **Sultans of Rome.** For in Asia the Eastern Empire had no name but that of Rome. Moreover the Christians in the Holy Land, and the pilgrims who went from Europe, were much worse treated by the Turks than they had been by the Saracens. So the Christians of the East prayed their brethren in the West to help them. In 1095 Pope **Urban the Second** held a Council at Clermont in Auvergne, where the holy war against the infidels was decreed. It was called a **Crusade**, because those who went on it put a cross on their shoulders, to show that they were the soldiers of Christ.

None of the kings of the West went on the first crusade, but many smaller princes and private men went, and in 1099 they took Jerusalem, and set up a kingdom of which **Godfrey** Duke of Lower Lotharingia was the first king. And now that the Turks were weakened, the Emperors of the house of **Komnênos, Alexios, John,** and **Manuel,** won back a great part of Asia. Manuel even helped Pope Alexander the Third and the Italian cities against the Emperor Frederick. For he hoped even now again to join the Old Rome and the New.

10. **The Later Crusades and the Latin Empire in the East.**—The strength of the kingdom of Jerusalem lay in the two orders called the **Templars** and the **Hospitallers** or Knights of Saint John. These were at once monks and soldiers; they took vows like monks and fought against the infidels. In 1147, the Second Crusade was preached by **Saint Bernard,** and King Conrad and King Lewis of France went to the Holy Land; but they did very little. Then in 1171 a new Mahometan power arose in Egypt, under Joseph called **Saladin,** who put down the Fatimites and brought Egypt again under the spiritual obedience of the Caliph of Bagdad. In 1187 he took Jerusalem and won nearly all Palestine from the Christians. And now the West was again moved. The Emperor Frederick went, but he was drowned on the way. And in 1190 King Philip of France and King **Richard** of England, called **Cœur de Lion** or Lion-Heart, both went. But the princes quarrelled, and little was done. Then in 1201 began the fourth crusade, which came to a strange end. The Eastern Empire had again fallen very low, and the princes who went on the crusade, **Henry Dandolo,** Doge or Duke of **Venice, Baldwin** Count of Flanders, and others, instead of going to the Holy Land, meddled in the revolutions of Constantinople, and in 1204 took the city. They set up Count Baldwin as the first of

the Latin Emperors of Constantinople. For all who belonged to the Western Church were called Latins as opposed to the Greeks. They divided as much of the Empire as they could, and the Venetians got many islands and havens. But Greek Emperors still reigned at Trebizond and Nikaia, and won back much of the land. At last in 1266, under the Emperor Michael Palaiologos, they got Constantinople again.

11. **Later Crusades in Palestine.**—Thus the fourth crusade did nothing for Christendom at all. But in 1228 the Emperor Frederick, who claimed the kingdom of Jerusalem in right of his wife, really won the Holy City by a treaty with the Egyptian Sultan Kamel. He was crowned, and reigned a little while. But even there Pope Gregory the Ninth and his other enemies would not let him alone, and so all was lost again. In 1244, Jerusalem was taken by another Mahometan people, the Chorasmians, and the Christians have never had it since. In 1248, Saint Lewis of France went, and in 1270 Edward of England, afterwards King Edward the First. But all that could be done was to save a few points in Palestine for a little while. At last, in 1291, Acre, the last Christian possession, was lost, and, though crusades were often talked of, nothing more was really done. A Latin kingdom of Cyprus had been set up in the third crusade, and the Venetians became an Eastern power in the fourth. But these conquests were made, not from the Mahometans, but from the Greeks.

12. **Mock Crusades.**—When the crusades had once begun, it was easy to turn them to other purposes. In the fourth crusade, Pope Innocent the Third tried to keep the crusaders from attacking Christians. But, before long, he and other Popes had crusades preached against Christians who were called heretics. This began with a crusade in 1208 against the people in the South of Gaul who were reckoned as

heretics, and who were called **Albigenses**, from the city of Alby. Cruel wars followed, and in the end Toulouse was added to France. Then crusades were preached against any enemies of the Popes, as the Emperor Frederick and his son **Manfred**, King of Sicily. Pope Urban the Fourth offered the crown of Sicily to the Count of Provence, **Charles of Anjou**. In 1266 Charles overcame Manfred and took the whole kingdom of Sicily; but in 1282 the people of the island of Sicily revolted, and chose Peter King of Aragon, Manfred's son-in-law. Thus the kingdom was divided; the French kings kept the mainland and the Aragonese kings kept the island. Both called themselves **Kings of Sicily**, but those on the mainland are better known as **Kings of Naples**.

13. **North-Eastern Europe**.—Another kind of crusade was also waged against the heathens on the Baltic. The **Prussians** and **Lithuanians** were still heathens, and so were the Finnish people in Livonia and Esthonia. Both Russia and Poland were thus cut off from the sea by their heathen neighbours. The Kings of Denmark made conquests on those coasts, but their advances were checked when, about 1230, the **Teutonic Knights**, a third order of military monks, settled in Prussia, and another branch of the order in Livonia. Their wars were reckoned as crusades, and men from other parts went to help them. But Christians and Mahometans, both in Europe and Asia, were soon threatened by a more terrible enemy than had been seen since Attila. These were the **Moguls** or **Tartars**, whose power began under Temujin or **Jenghiz Khan** in 1206. They were at first neither Christians nor Mahometans, but, as they settled down in Persia and elsewhere, they gradually became Mahometans. One of their princes, **Batou**, pressed into Europe as far as the borders of Poland and Germany. But the only part of Europe where they settled was in **Russia**. The Khans at Kasan held

the Russian princes in dependence, and the **Lithuanians** were thus able to conquer all western Russia, with the old capital of Kiev. Thus Russia was thrown back for many ages. The Moguls also in 1258 put an end to the Caliphate at Bagdad, though a line of nominal Caliphs still went on in Egypt. In one way the Moguls helped Christendom; for they broke up the power of the Seljuk Turks, and so saved the Greek states at Nikaia and Trebizond.

14. **Summary.**—During this time both the Empires, Eastern and Western, really came to an end. Their titles went on, but they were no longer the two great powers of Europe. The two Mahometan Caliphates also came to an end. The Western was broken up into small kingdoms, till only Granada was left. The Eastern was first broken up by the Turks, and then swept away by the Moguls. Thus there was no longer, among either Christians or Mahometans, any universal temporal power. Europe, and the neighbouring parts of Asia and Africa, now formed groups of independent states, over which the Emperors and Caliphs kept no real power. And as the Emperors grew weaker, the Popes grew stronger. Christendom grew at one end by the recovery of Spain and Sicily, and lost at the other end by the conquests of the Turks from the Eastern Empire and by the establishment of the Mogul power over Russia. Castile was the chief power of Spain, and France, after a struggle with the Norman and Angevin Kings of England, became the chief power of Gaul. In Germany and Italy the Imperial power was weakened, to the gain of the princes in Germany and of the cities in Italy. The kingdom of Sicily grew up and split into two. The Eastern Empire was broken into a crowd of small states, Greek and Frank, and the Eastern power of Venice began. On the Baltic the Teutonic Knights hindered the eastern growth of Denmark and in some sort began the power of Prussia. In short, the

thirteenth century was an age of endings and beginnings throughout Europe and Asia, and in most parts of Europe things now began to grow into the shape in which they are still.

CHAPTER VIII.

THE DECLINE OF THE TWO EMPIRES.

1. **The Habsburg and Lüzelburg Kings.—** After Frederick the Second the power of the Western Empire went down. Some kings were never crowned Emperors, and those who were crowned kept no real hold on Italy. The greater part of Burgundy was swallowed up by France. Even in Germany, the royal power grew less and less. After **Conrad's** death, from 1254 to 1273, came the **Great Interregnum**, when no one king was acknowledged everywhere. In 1256, **Richard** of Cornwall, brother of our Henry the Third, and Alfonso of Castile, were both chosen kings, and Richard was crowned. But he lived chiefly in England. In 1274, when he died, **Rudolf** Count of Habsburg was chosen, and did much to bring back law and order. He gave the Duchy of Austria to his son **Albert**, who was afterwards King. Then the **House of Austria** began. The next King, **Henry the Seventh** of Lüzelburg or Luxemburg, who reigned from 1308 to 1313, was crowned Emperor at Rome, which no King since Frederick the Second had been, and he seemed likely to win back all the old power of the Empire. After him the Emperors had no real power in Italy. Several of Henry's descendants were Kings and Emperors for nearly a hundred years, from 1346 to 1437. They also became Kings of Bohemia and Hungary. Then, in 1437, came another **Albert** of Austria. Thus the

Kingdoms of Hungary and Bohemia and the Duchy of Austria came to be specially connected with the Empire. Indeed, from Albert onwards, for three hundred years, an Austrian prince was always chosen. The last Emperor who was crowned at Rome was Frederick the Third in 1452.

2. **The Popes and the Councils.**—The Papacy too next began to go down as well as the Empire. **Boniface the Eighth,** who reigned from 1294 to 1303, tried to rule like the former Popes; but the King of the French, **Philip the Fair,** sent and seized him, and afterwards had a creature of his own, **Clement the Fifth,** chosen. Then the Popes left Rome and lived till 1376 at Avignon, just outside the French border. In 1378 two Popes were chosen, **Urban the Sixth** and **Clement the Seventh:** so Urban lived at Rome and Clement at Avignon. In 1409 a General Council, that is an Assembly of Bishops of the whole Western Church, met at **Pisa** to settle this dispute. They deposed both Popes and chose a third; and then in 1415 King Siegmund, who was afterwards Emperor, held a Council at **Constanz,** which got rid of all the Popes, and chose **Martin the Fifth.** From 1431 to 1439 another Council at **Basel** tried, but in vain, to lessen the power of the Popes and to strengthen that of national churches.

3. **The Italian Cities.**—Now that the Emperor had lost all real power in Italy, the land formed a group of separate states, like those of old Greece, some of them being commonwealths and some ruled by Princes. Some one man often made himself master of his own city, and perhaps of several others, and handed on his power to his children. But such men were called **Lords** or **Tyrants.** To give a show of right, they often got the Emperor or the Pope to grant them their dominions as a fief, with the title of Duke or Marquess. Thus many cities changed into principalities. At Milan the power of the

Visconti gradually grew up, and in 1395 the then King **Wenceslaus** made their dominions into the **Duchy of Milan**. The other chief state of Northern Italy was the oligarchic commonwealth of **Venice**, which, besides its power in the East, gained in the fourteenth century a great dominion on the mainland. **Genoa** also was still a commonwealth, and powerful by sea. In the thirteenth century **Florence** became great, and was the chief example of a democracy. But she too had subject cities, and, during the great part of the fifteenth century, she ruled over **Pisa**. But in the fifteenth century the **Medici** began to gain the chief power, though, as under Augustus at Rome, the forms of the commonwealth went on. Florence was also the chief seat of commerce, literature and art. No one city ever had more great men, the famous poet **Dante Alighieri** among the foremost.

4. **The Popes and the Sicilian Kings.**—Meanwhile at the other end of Italy the two Sicilian kingdoms went on, on the mainland and on the island. After the French were driven out of the island, it was ruled by Kings of the House of Aragon, but, after the first King **Frederick**, it was of no account, and after a while it was joined to Aragon. In the kingdom on the mainland, or kingdom of Naples, there were long disputes as to the succession. During the greater part of the fifteenth century its crown also was held by Kings of the House of **Aragon**; but it was claimed, and now and then won, by the Dukes of **Anjou**, whose claims at last passed to the Kings of France. Meanwhile in central Italy the Popes were growing up into a new temporal power. While they lived at Avignon, there was utter confusion at Rome, save when in 1347 **Cola di Rienzi** set up a commonwealth for a moment and ruled as Tribune. But after the Popes had come back, and had got the better of the Councils, they thought chiefly of enlarging their temporal power; and, during all the latter part of the

fifteenth century, they were little more than Italian princes.

5. **England, France, and Scotland.**—During the thirteenth century all the people of England had become united, and had won their freedom from the kings. Then came the reign of **Edward the First**, whose great object, like that of the old kings, was to join together all Britain; and then came the long wars with France. The French kings were always trying to get Aquitaine; and, when the enmity between England and Scotland began, Scotland and France always helped one another against England. At last the great war called the **Hundred Years' War** began between **Edward the Third** of England and the French king **Philip of Valois**. Philip was aiming at Aquitaine, and in return Edward claimed the crown of France in right of his mother. Ever since Hugh Capet, a male heir had never been wanting, so that men said that the Crown could never pass through a woman. Then came the great victories of **Crecy** in 1346 and **Poitiers** in 1356, and in 1360, by the Peace of **Bretigny**, Edward gave up his claim to the French Crown, but became independent prince of Aquitaine, Calais, and some other districts. But the French soon broke the treaty, and, before Edward died in 1377, nearly all Aquitaine was lost, except the cities of Bourdeaux and Bayonne. After this there was no peace for a long while, but there were many truces, and the war went on feebly till **Henry the Fifth** of England began it again in good earnest. The French king Charles the Sixth was weak, or rather mad, and the land was full of confusion. In 1415 Henry won the Battle of **Agincourt**, and in 1420, by the Treaty of **Troyes**, it was settled that Henry should succeed on the death of Charles, and that the crowns of England and France should be for ever united. But both Charles and Henry died soon after; the treaty was not carried out, and the war went on between **Henry the**

Sixth of England and **Charles the Seventh** of France. At last, in 1453, the English were driven out of all France and Aquitaine, and kept only Calais.

6. The Growth of France.—Notwithstanding these wars, France was growing all this time. The kings were increasing their power in their own dominions, they were annexing the dominions of their vassals, and they were winning lands beyond their own kingdom. In the fourteenth and fifteenth centuries the French kings got possession of most of the Kingdom of Burgundy. In 1314 **Philip the Fair** got hold of the imperial city of **Lyons**. In 1349, Charles, the eldest son of King John of France, bought the land of **Vienne**, which was called the **Dauphiny**, and from that time the eldest son of the King of France was called the Dauphin. And in 1481 **Lewis the Eleventh** annexed **Provence** to France. Thus all the land between the Rhône and the Alps was swallowed up, save only Orange, which kept its own princes, and Avignon and Venaissin, which belonged to the Popes. Thus the French kingdom was greatly enlarged, and within the kingdom all the great fiefs were joined to the crown, save only Britanny and Flanders.

7. Switzerland and Burgundy.—While the Empire was getting weaker and more divided, and while France was getting stronger and more united, two new powers arose in the border-land between them. These were the League of the Swiss Cantons and the Duchy of Burgundy. The German cities and free districts often made Leagues like those of old Greece, but one of these Leagues grew to a special importance in the fourteenth century. This was the League of the **Three Lands, Uri, Schwyz** and **Unterwalden**, on the borders of Germany, Burgundy and Italy. These little mountain lands had kept much more of the old freedom than most other parts of Germany. They were in favour with the Swabian Emperors, but, when their neighbours the Counts of Habsburg became Dukes of Austria, they had to fight for their freedom against them. They secured it in 1315 by the battle of **Morgarten**, in which they overthrew the Austrian Duke Leopold. Then the neighbouring cities, **Luzern**, **Zürich**, and **Bern** joined them, and they formed a League of eight Cantons called the **Old League of High Germany**. But from the land of **Schwyz** they came to be called **Swiss**. The League had still to defend itself against the Dukes of Austria and other enemies; but it grew, and the Cantons became the chiefs of many allies and subjects. Meanwhile the power of the **Dukes of Burgundy** was growing up. These were a branch of the French royal family, who first held the French Duchy of Burgundy, and gradually added to it many other fiefs, both of France, like the County of Flanders, and of the Empire, like the County of Burgundy. Thus Duke **Philip the Good**, who reigned from 1419 to 1469, was, because of his border position, one of the great princes of Europe. His son, **Charles the Bold**, had a great rivalry with Lewis the Eleventh of France, and made enemies on all sides, the Confederates among them. A war followed in 1476, in which the Confederates overthrew Duke Charles in two battles in the Savoyard lands, at **Granson** and **Morat**. Next year he was defeated and killed at **Nancy** in Lorraine. His dominion was broken up; the Duchy of Burgundy was annexed to France, and there was no longer a great middle power between France and Germany. The Confederates got great fame and began to spread their dominion over their Romance neighbours. But unluckily they also took to serving for hire in foreign armies, especially in France.

8. **The Spanish Kingdoms.**—Though the Mahometans in Spain were now shut up in the one kingdom of Granada, they kept their ground till

the end of the fifteenth century. For the Spanish kingdoms were often at war with one another, and **Aragon** was much mixed up with the affairs of France and Italy. The wars between the Aragonese and the Angevin kings of Naples sometimes spread into Aragon itself. At last Castile and Aragon were united in 1471 by the marriage of **Ferdinand** of Aragon with **Isabel** of Castile. In 1492 Granada was taken, and the Mahometan power in Spain came to an end. Before long, all that part of the kingdom of **Navarre** which lay south of the Pyrenees was conquered. Thus the kings of **Castile and Aragon** reigned over the whole peninsula, except Portugal, and they were commonly spoken of as **Kings of Spain**. Spain presently grew to be the first power in Europe. But meanwhile **Portugal** was doing great things in another way; for her princes in the fifteenth century, especially the Infant **Don Henry**, made voyages of discovery and settlement both in Africa and the islands in the Atlantic. This was the beginning of European trade and settlements in distant lands; Portugal began, and other nations followed. In 1486 the discovery of the Cape of Good Hope opened a still wider field in India and elsewhere, first for Portugal and afterwards for other nations.

9. **The fall of the Eastern Empire.**—While the Mahometans were thus driven out of Western Europe, they were gaining ground wonderfully in the East. After the Greeks had won back Constantinople, the Empire was a mere shadow of its old self; yet the Emperors of the House of **Palaiologos** were able to join to it many of the little states, Greek and Frank, which had arisen out of the Latin Conquest. And whenever the Greeks were hard pressed, there was always some show of uniting the Eastern and Western Churches. The Empire and all Christendom were now threatened by a more dangerous Mahometan enemy than any since the time of

the first Saracens. These were a new race of Turks, the **Ottomans**, who began to rise to power in the latter part of the thirteenth century. They gradually swallowed up the Asiatic provinces of the Empire; then in 1343 they got a footing in Europe, and in 1361 their Sultan **Amurath** took Hadrianople and made it his capital. Thus Constantinople was quite hemmed in, and nothing was left to the Empire but some outlying points in Macedonia and Greece. But the Empire was saved for a moment by the rise of a new power in Asia, that of **Timour**, whose descendants are commonly called Moguls, though they were in truth rather Turks. He was a Mahometan of the Shiah sect, and was as fierce against orthodox Mahometans as against Christians. He therefore attacked the Ottoman power in Asia, and took the Sultan Bajazet prisoner in 1402. He never crossed into Europe; and, as a civil war followed among the Ottomans, the Empire got a breathing time. At last, in 1453, Constantinople was taken by the Sultan **Mahomet the Conqueror**; the last Emperor, **Constantine Palaiologos**, died fighting, and the Roman Empire of the East came to an end. Mahomet presently conquered Peloponnêsos and the Empire of Trebizond. Thus the Turks became a great power in Europe, and in a manner took the place of the Eastern Empire. But the Venetians, the Knights of St. John, and other Latin powers, still kept several islands and points on the coasts of Greece and Asia.

10. **Russia, Poland, and Hungary.**—Meanwhile other parts of Europe had Mahometan enemies to deal with. Long before the Ottomans had taken Constantinople, they had spread their power over the countries to the north, as **Servia** and **Bulgaria**, and this brought them into the neighbourhood of **Hungary** and **Poland**. These last nations became the great bulwarks of Christendom by land, as Venice was by sea. In 1396, **Siegmund**, King of Hungary, the same who was afterwards Emperor, with many

VIII.]   *END OF THE EASTERN EMPIRE.*   93

crusaders from the West, was overthrown by the Sultan Bajazet at Nikopolis. Meanwhile in 1386, **Jagellon** Duke of Lithuania had embraced Christianity along with his people, and had married **Hedwig**, Queen of Poland. Thus Poland and Lithuania, with the large part of Russia which they had conquered, formed a very powerful state. Jagellon's son **Vladislaus** was also King of Hungary. He drove back Sultan Amurath for a while, but in 1444 he was defeated and slain at **Varna**. But the Turks were kept in check by **John Huniades**, Prince of Transilvania and Regent of Hungary, and his son, **Matthias Corvinus**, who was King of Hungary, and who, besides the Turks, had to keep the House of Austria in check at the other end of his kingdom. Meanwhile in 1466 Poland got the better of the Teutonic Knights, and annexed the western part of **Prussia**. Russia, while cut short by Poland to the West, was held in bondage by the Moguls to the East. But she gradually gained strength, and at last was set free in 1477. But the Mahometans still kept the lands on the north of the Euxine, just as the Saracens in Spain had kept Granada.

11. **The Scandinavian Kingdoms.**—In 1397 the three Scandinavian kingdoms were all joined under Queen **Margaret**, daughter of Waldemar the Third of Denmark. This is called the **Union of Calmar.** Had it lasted, a very great power might have been founded in the North, but the union was often broken, and it came to an end before very long. Denmark had now quite sunk from its former power on the Baltic coasts. In 1448, under Christian the First, the House of **Oldenburg** began to reign, which has reigned in Denmark ever since, and in Norway till quite lately. All the Scandinavian kingdoms had many wars with the League of the **Hanse Towns,** the trading cities of Northern Germany, which had become a great power in the Baltic.

12. **The Revival of Learning.**—During these centuries most of the modern languages of Europe came nearly to their present form. English, which after the Norman Conquest, had ceased to be a polite language, became once more in the fourteenth century the one language of England. In French there were many good writers, both in France and England; but the advance of the French power in Southern Gaul caused the Provençal tongue to be thrust down to be a mere popular speech, as it is still. The Italian tongue came to its perfection in the latter part of the thirteenth century under **Dante Alighieri.** Meanwhile the learning of the older times was growing again. In the twelfth century many men studied the Latin writers, also such philosophy as was then known, and also the Roman law, which last study greatly helped the cause of the Swabian Emperors in Italy. From that time learning steadily grew; but Greek was not much studied till, in the last days of the Eastern Empire, many learned men from Constantinople sought shelter in Italy, and from Italy the revived learning spread itself into other lands. And with it came a taste for the old Greek and Roman models in architecture and other arts. But both in literature and in architecture the imitation of the past checked original power. Many of the Popes and other Italian princes were great patrons of art and learning, which has sometimes made men forget the evils of their rule and the wickedness of their lives.

13. **Summary.**—Thus, between the middle of the thirteenth and the middle of the fifteenth century, both Empires really came to an end. The Eastern Empire was swallowed up by the Turks; the Western Empire lost all its power, and an Emperor was crowned at Rome for the last time. A great Mahometan power arose in South-Eastern Europe, which has ever since held several Christian nations in bondage. On the other hand, Spain got rid of the last Mahometan kingdom in Western

Europe, and Russia set herself free from the Mahometans in the North-East. The long wars between England and France began and ended, and France greatly strengthened herself by annexing the lands both of her vassals and of her neighbours. The two middle states, Burgundy and Switzerland, arose, of which Switzerland lasted, while Burgundy came to an end. In Italy most of the commonwealths fell under tyrants who grew into princes, and the Popes became mere Italian sovereigns. The Scandinavian kingdoms were united, though not very firmly. Poland grew into a great power, and shared with Hungary and Venice the work of defending Christendom against the Turks.

CHAPTER IX.

THE REFORMATION AND THE RELIGIOUS WARS.

1. **Beginnings of Modern Europe.**—We now come to **Modern History**, to the beginning of the state of things which goes on still. The great powers of the older time, the two Empires and the two Caliphates, have passed away in fact, though not altogether in name. We have now chiefly to do, neither with empires nor with nations, but with great royal houses, each of which had inherited or conquered several older kingdoms or other states. Governments now grew more powerful, and the disorders of the old times came to an end; but in most countries the way in which governments grew more powerful was by the princes overthrowing the old freedom. Kings now began to keep **standing armies**, that is, soldiers always paid and kept under arms, whereas of old both princes and commonwealths had called on all their people to fight

when they were wanted. Thus the Kings were able to do as they pleased, and in many lands the National Assemblies came to an end. Moreover, three things now became commonly known which have changed the face of the world. These were **printing**, which made it much easier to gain knowledge; **gunpowder**, which brought in a new manner of warfare; and the **mariner's compass**, which enabled men to make longer voyages, and so led to the discovery of distant lands. It was, in short, a time when a new world was found out, and when the greatest changes were going on in the old world.

2. **The Reformation of Religion.**—But, above all, this was the time of the greatest changes in religious matters. There had been movements in this way ever since the thirteenth century. Many men had taught doctrines which the Western Church called heretical, and many men had been burned for holding such doctrines. The Albigenses had been put down by a Crusade, and the like was done in the fifteenth century with the followers of **John Huss** in Bohemia. But in the sixteenth century men began more generally to question the received doctrines, especially to revolt against the powers of the Bishops of Rome. Both Old and New Rome had come to be the head cities of the Church, because they were the head cities of the Empire; but now that the temporal power of Rome had passed away, the time seemed come for its spiritual power to pass away too. The Popes also often used their power badly, and greatly meddled with the rights of national governments and churches. There were also many abuses in the Church which the Popes might easily have reformed. But, instead of this, they withstood all attempts at reform, whether they were made by the General Councils or by the governments of particular countries. Moreover many men thought that much **that was** taught and done was wrong **in itself**, and

had no ground in Scripture or the early Church. So, in the course of the sixteenth century, a large part of Western Europe threw off the Pope's dominion, and each nation made such changes in religion as it thought right. Speaking roughly, the Teutonic nations threw off the Pope's dominion, while the Romance nations clave to it. The Eastern Church was now hardly thought of; for the Greeks and their neighbours were under the Turks, and Russia was not yet of any account.

3. **Growth of the Spanish Power.**—During the sixteenth century Spain was the greatest power in Europe. For Ferdinand held the whole Spanish peninsula except Portugal, with Sardinia and the island of Sicily; and he won the kingdom of Naples on the mainland. His daughter Joanna married Philip the son of Maximilian of Austria and of Mary the daughter of Charles the Bold. Their son **Charles** thus inherited kingdoms and duchies from each of his parents and grand-parents, and, besides the dominions of Ferdinand and Isabel, he held the Netherlands and the county of Burgundy. In 1519 he was chosen Emperor as **Charles the Fifth**. Thus the Emperor was again the most powerful prince in Europe, but his main power came, not from the Empire, but from his own dominions. Charles gave up his crowns in 1555, and was succeeded in the Empire by his brother Ferdinand; but the chief power in Europe passed to Charles' son **Philip the Second**, who succeeded him in his hereditary dominions. Philip reigned till 1598. In 1580 he won Portugal, so that the whole Spanish peninsula was united. But in 1639 Portugal became independent again, under the house of **Braganza.** After Philip's death, the power of Spain greatly went down. The Spanish Kings were the most bigoted and despotic in Europe. The Reformation was trampled out in Spain itself, and the attempt to do so in

E. Pr. G

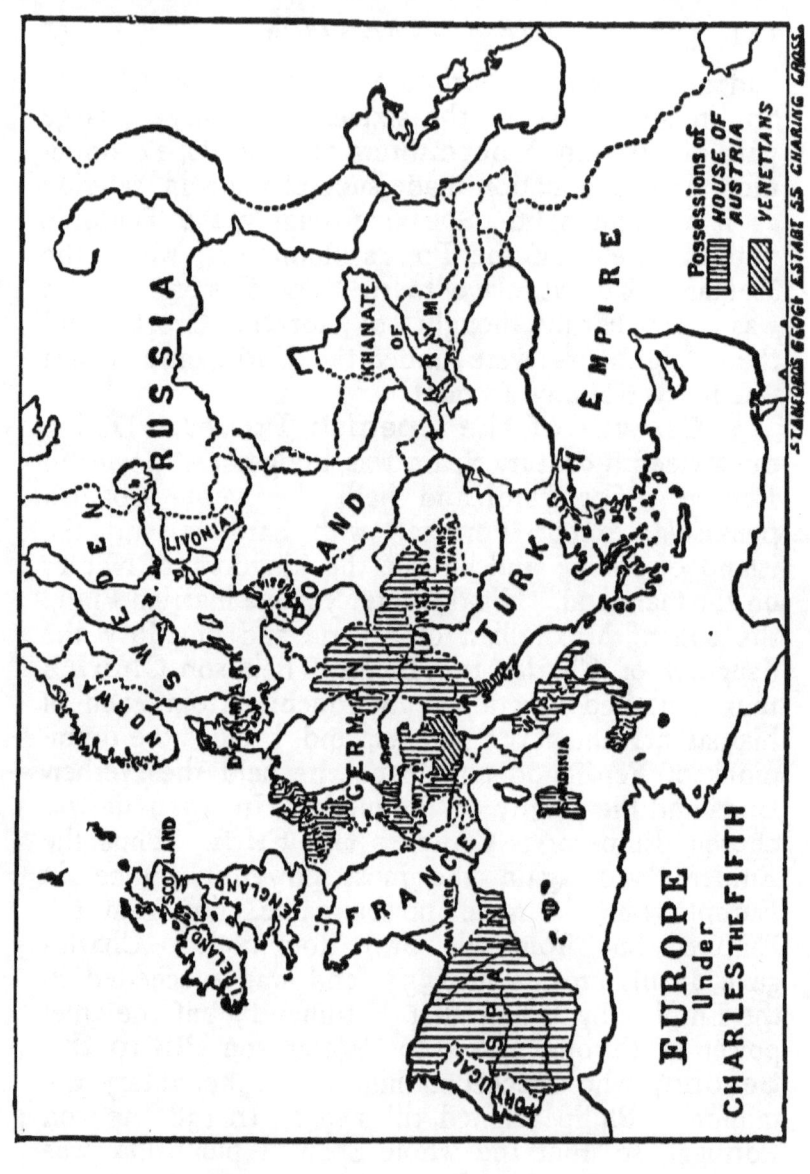

the Netherlands led to the loss of seven of those provinces. Moreover, the descendants of the Mahometans of Granada were driven out of Spain.

4. **The Wars of Italy.**—Meanwhile in Italy the old rivalry between the Houses of Anjou and Aragon grew into a greater rivalry between France and Spain. In 1494 **Charles the Eighth** of France marched all through Italy, won the kingdom of Naples, and lost it again directly. The next King, Lewis the Twelfth, claimed the Duchy of Milan as well as Naples; he took Milan, and agreed to divide the kingdom of Naples with Ferdinand; but presently, in 1504, Ferdinand took it all to himself. Then in 1508 Lewis and Ferdinand, with Pope **Julius the Second** and the Emperor-elect **Maximilian**, made the **League of Cambray** to despoil the Republic of Venice. But they quarrelled among themselves, and Venice got back nearly all that she had lost. From this time the war went on till 1529, first between Ferdinand and Lewis, and then between their successors, Charles in Spain and **Francis the First** in France. Milan was taken over and over again, and at last Charles gave it to his son Philip. In 1525 Francis was taken prisoner at the **battle of Pavia**; in 1527 **Rome** was sacked by the Imperial troops, and at last, in 1529, peace was made. Next year Charles was crowned at Bologna both as King of Italy and as Emperor, since which time no Emperor has been crowned in Italy. When Charles abdicated, his power in Italy passed to his son Philip of Spain.

5. **The Commonwealths of Italy.**—During these wars the greatness of the commonwealths of Italy came to an end. At Florence, the Medici, who had grown into tyrants, were driven out and brought back over and over again, according to the chances of war. For France professed to be the ally of the commonwealth, while two of the Popes of the time, **Leo the Tenth** and **Clement the Seventh**, were

of the house of the Medici, and did all that they could for their kinsmen. When peace was made in 1529, Francis forsook his allies, and Florence was left alone. Then the Pope and the Emperor joined against her, and she was obliged to receive the Medici as **Dukes**. Presently Duke Cosmo added the commonwealth of Siena to his dominions, and the **Grand Duchy of Tuscany** was thus made. The only commonwealths left now were Venice, Lucca, Genoa, and little San Marino; and Venice was now the only one which played any great part. She was one of the great bulwarks of Christendom against the Turks; and in 1570 the Spanish and Venetian fleets won the battle of **Lepanto**, the first great check to the Ottoman power. Yet Venice had to give up **Cyprus**, but she still kept Crete and several smaller islands.

6. **The Popes.**—At the beginning of the sixteenth century the Popes meddled greatly in the wars of Italy to increase their temporal dominions or to provide for their kinsfolk. Some of them were men of most wicked lives, especially **Alexander the Sixth**, of the Spanish house of Borgia. **Leo the Tenth** got great fame as a patron of learning and art, but he was really little better than the others. In his time **Martin Luther** began to preach the Reformation in Germany, but for a long time the Popes took little heed to what was going on. The Reformation was never accepted by any part of Italy, though many men were anxious to make particular reforms. The Popes in the latter part of the century were mostly another kind of men; fierce bigots, but men of good lives, and eager for what they thought their duty. Between 1545 and 1563 sat the famous **Council of Trent**, which reformed many practical evils, but fixed the Roman Catholic creed in so rigid a shape that there was no longer any hope of the Popes and the Reformers coming to an agreement. From this time Western Christendom

was finally divided. Towards the end of the century the Roman Church won back no small part of the lands which had thrown off its obedience. This was chiefly done by the **Jesuits**, or **Order of Jesus**, founded by the Spaniard **Ignatius Loyola**.

7. **The Reformation in Germany.**—After Frederick the Third, his son **Maximilian** took the new titles of **Emperor-elect** and **King of Germany**. But the German Kings were now commonly called Emperors, though none after Charles the Fifth went into Italy to be crowned. Maximilian tried to bring Germany into better order, and towards the end of his reign, in 1517, **Luther** began to preach the Reformed doctrines. Hence came great religious dissensions in Germany, and civil wars. Charles the Fifth was now chosen Emperor, and the Reformers were condemned in two Diets, at **Worms** in 1521 and at **Speyer** in 1529. But at Speyer the princes and cities that followed Luther protested against the decree, whence the name of **Protestants** was given to the Reformers, first in Germany and afterwards elsewhere. At last, in 1555, by the **Peace of Augsburg**, the two religions were put on a level throughout Germany. That is to say, each prince or city might establish either religion at pleasure. But this gave no toleration to those who differed from the religion of their own prince or city. Thus in Austria, where the people had largely become Protestant, while the Archdukes remained Catholic, the Catholic religion was brought back by the Jesuits. After the abdication of Charles, his brother Ferdinand, King of the Romans, succeeded him as Emperor-elect. The Empire was now almost wholly German. The chief power in Italy had passed to Spain, and the greater part of Burgundy had been swallowed up by France.

8. **The Advance of France.**—The rivalry between France and Spain, which began in the wars of Italy, went on between the French Kings and the two

branches of the **House of Austria**; that is, the Emperors of that House and the Austrian Kings of Spain. In Italy the French Kings could not keep either Milan or Naples; but the war went on, and, while Francis and his son Henry the Second persecuted the Protestants in France, they encouraged the Protestants of Germany against the Emperor, and even encouraged the Turks to attack the Empire. In 1552 France made its first conquest at the expense of Germany by winning the Three Bishopricks of **Metz, Toul,** and **Verdun,** which were surrounded by the Duchy of Lorraine. At last in 1558 peace was made at **Câteau Cambresis**; and from 1562, for about thirty years, the advance of France was checked by the religious wars. The **Huguenots** or French Protestants were followers of the French Reformer **John Chauvin** or **Calvin,** who settled at Geneva. His teaching, which went much further from the Roman Church than that of Luther, was followed by such of the Romance-speaking lands as accepted the Reformation, and by some parts of Germany. After Henry the Second, three of his sons, Francis the Second, Charles the Ninth, and Henry the Third, reigned from 1559 to 1589. Under Charles the Ninth in 1572, was the **Massacre of Saint Bartholomew,** when many of the Huguenots were slain in Paris. During the latter part of these wars, the Huguenot leader was **Henry of Bourbon,** King of Navarre, that is, of the little piece of Navarre north of the Pyrenees. He was next heir to the French crown after the sons of Henry the Second; and, when Henry the Third was killed, the crown came to him. But Paris and a great part of France would not acknowledge him till he turned Catholic in 1593. He was murdered in 1610. Then came his son Lewis the Thirteenth, under whose minister **Cardinal Richelieu** the royal power was firmly established, and France began to take the first place in Europe.

9. **The Revolt of the Netherlands.**—Meanwhile the power of Spain received a great blow, and a new commonwealth arose. The **Netherlands**, as part of the possessions of the Dukes of Burgundy, had passed to Philip of Spain, and his bigotry caused great discontents. In 1568 a revolt began under William of Nassau, called **William the Silent.** He was a Prince of the Empire, as having inherited the little principality of Orange which was now almost surrounded by France, and he was the chief man in the Netherlands. The seven northern provinces were now set free from Spain, and were formed in 1581 into a federal commonwealth called the **Seven United Provinces**, of which **Holland** was the greatest. But Philip and his successors kept the southern provinces, where the people were mostly Catholics. In 1584 the Prince of Orange was murdered, but the war was carried on by his son **Maurice**, till a truce with Spain, which was really a peace, was made in 1609. The Provinces remained nominally members of the Empire till 1648; but they were really independent both of the Empire and of Spain. And though the territory of the **Dutch**, as we call the people of the Seven Provinces in a special way, was so small, yet their courage and energy, especially by sea, was so great that, all through the seventeenth century, their confederation was reckoned as one of the chief powers of Europe.

10. **Switzerland and Savoy.**—Meanwhile the older League at the other end of the Empire, the old League of High Germany, whose people were now called the **Swiss**, grew greatly after the war with Charles of Burgundy. They took in five new cantons, making in all thirteen, all German; but they had now allies and subjects in the Romance-speaking lands. The Confederates took a great part in the Italian wars, and won part of Lombardy, which is now the canton of Ticino. But their power chiefly grew in the

old kingdom of Burgundy. The only great princes there who had not fallen under the power of France were the **Dukes of Savoy**. They had lands on both sides of the Alps, and, from that time till now, their house has lost ground on the Burgundian side and gained it on the Italian. The Swiss had their own Reformation distinct from that of Germany; its leader was **Ulrich Zwingli** of Zürich, who began to preach in 1519. Bern and Zürich and some other parts accepted his teaching, but others, and the old Three Lands among them, remained Catholic. Meanwhile William Farel preached at **Geneva**, which was in alliance with Bern and others cantons. The Dukes of Savoy, by whose dominions Geneva was hemmed in, often tried to seize it. But Geneva was helped by her allies, and the Dukes of Savoy lost all their lands north of the lake and some to the south, but these last were given back in 1564. Thus Bern and others of the Confederates and their allies won a dominion in the Romance lands. Geneva remained free, and became the dwelling-place of Calvin and the chief place of his teaching. From this time the Dukes of Savoy had mainly to do with Italy. In 1648 the Swiss Cantons were formally acknowledged as independent of the Empire.

11. **England and Scotland.**—Meanwhile in our own island the Reformation was accepted in different forms both in England and in Scotland, and the two crowns were joined together. The latter half of the fifteenth century in England was full of the civil wars between the Houses of York and Lancaster. **Henry the Eighth**, in 1509, was the first King whose title was undisputed. In his time religious changes began. He threw off the authority of the Pope, but those who taught the Reformed doctrines were still burned. More strictly religious changes began under Edward the Sixth; but his sister Mary, who married Philip of Spain, brought back not only the old religion, but the

authority of the Popes. Under **Elizabeth**, who began to reign in 1558, the English Church was finally reformed. The Pope was again got rid of, but less change was made than in other lands; while in Scotland, where the Reformation began later than in England, greater changes were made than anywhere else. For in England the King began to make changes, and in Scotland the people. But the Queen of Scots, **Mary Stewart**, who had been the wife of Francis the Second of France, stuck to the old religion. She was driven out of her kingdom, and sought shelter in England in 1569. Eighteen years after she was beheaded for her share in a plot against Elizabeth. Then in 1588 Philip of Spain sent his **Armada** or Great Fleet to conquer England, which came to nothing. Elizabeth was now the head of the Protestant party throughout Europe, and the war with Spain went on all her days. On her death, in 1603, **James the Sixth** of Scotland succeeded her in England, so France could no longer count on Scotland as an ally against England. England now lost the place which she held in Europe under Elizabeth. Under Charles the First came the **Great Civil War** between the King and the Parliament, and, under the Protector **Oliver Cromwell**, England again became a great power.

12. **Northern Europe.**—Early in the sixteenth century the union of the three Scandinavian kingdoms came altogether to an end. **Christian** the Second, called **the Cruel**, reigned for a while over all three. In 1523 Sweden and Denmark chose different kings. Sweden chose **Gustavus Vasa**, who brought in the doctrines of Luther; but in Sweden, as in England, much less change was made than elsewhere. Sweden now took a higher position in Europe than it had done before, especially under its greatest King, **Gustavus Adolphus**. Under his daughter Christina the Swedish frontier was enlarged westwards.

Meanwhile the **Oldenburg Kings** reigned over both Denmark and Norway. Under Frederick the First, who reigned from 1523 to 1533, the Lutheran religion was established in Denmark, and Frederick the Second, from 1559 to 1588, conquered the land of **Dithmarschen**, where the people had still kept the old freedom, as the Forest Cantons had done at the other end of Germany.

13. **Poland and Prussia.**—In the sixteenth century, under the House of **Jagellon**, Poland was one of the greatest states of Europe, stretching over a great part of Russia. But part of the Russian territory was presently lost, and since then the Polish frontier has gone back. In 1525 the Teutonic Knights were abolished, and their Grand Master **Albert of Brandenburg** became hereditary **Duke of East Prussia**, as a vassal of Poland. Presently the Duchy of Prussia was joined with the Electorate of Brandenburg; afterwards Prussia was released from its vassalage, and Brandenburg and Prussia together formed a new power. So part of the possessions of the Knights in **Livonia** were added, first to Poland and then to Sweden, and part was made into a Duchy by the Grand Master Kettler. In 1573 the crown of Poland was made purely elective, and from that time the power of the country greatly went down.

14. **Russia.**—Meanwhile Russia, which had been so long in the background, was growing up again. Under John or Ivan the Fourth, called **Ivan the Terrible**, who reigned from 1533 to 1584, the Tartars of Kasan were utterly overthrown, and the Russian frontier reached to the Caspian Sea. But from the Euxine Russia was cut off by the Tartars of Krim, who answered to the Spanish Saracens at Granada. From the Baltic Russia was cut off by Poland and Sweden, so that all the trade that Russia had with Western Europe was by the White Sea. Ivan took the title of Czar, which some say is a

corruption of **Cæsar**, for the rulers of Russia have always wished to be deemed the successors of the Eastern Emperors. In 1589 the line of Ruric came to an end, and, after a time of confusion, the house of **Romanoff** began in 1613. Since then Russia has steadily pressed eastward, westward, and southward.

15. **Turkey and Hungary.**—In the first year of the sixteenth century the Ottomans were threatened by a fresh Mahometan enemy. As Persia had before risen under Artaxerxes by the preaching of the old Persian religion, it rose again now under princes called the Sophis, by the preaching of the **Shiah** form of Mahometanism. Meanwhile the Ottomans were pressing westward, northward, and southward. **Selim the Inflexible**, who reigned from 1512 to 1520, won Syria and Egypt, and the nominal Caliph in Egypt gave up his rights to him. This made the Ottoman Sultan the head of all orthodox Mahometans. Then from 1520 to 1566 came **Suleiman** —that is, Solomon—**the Lawgiver**, under whom the Ottoman power greatly advanced. In his war with the Emperor Charles he was backed up by Francis of France. The greater part of Hungary was conquered, Vienna was besieged, the Knights of Saint John were driven from Rhodes and afterwards besieged in Malta, which had been given them by the Emperor. Suleiman was the last of the Sultans who threatened the whole world, but after his time the Turks still made some conquests. They had endless wars with Persia to the east, and with Poland and Hungary to the north. From this time, beginning with the Emperor Ferdinand, the Hungarian crown has always been held by Austrian princes.

16. **The Thirty Years' War.**—Out of the religious disputes of the sixteenth century came the great religious war of the seventeenth century, called the **Thirty Years' War**, which was waged in Germany, but in which many other nations took a share. It

began in Bohemia in 1619, where the intolerance of the King, the Emperor **Ferdinand the Second**, drove the Protestants to revolt, and they chose **Frederick the Elector Palatine** to be King. Frederick lost both his new kingdom and his old dominions; but the war spread through all Germany. At first the Imperial troops carried all before them; so other Protestant powers stepped in, **Christian the Fourth** of Denmark first, and then **Gustavus Adolphus** of Sweden. He came in 1630, and won great victories for two years, and then was killed at **Lützen**. But Sweden took a part in the war till the end. So far the war had been for the defence of Protestantism in Germany; but in 1635, France under Richelieu joined in it, and it became a war for the aggrandizement of France. Peace was made 1648 under a new Emperor, **Ferdinand the Third**, who began in 1637, and a new King of France, **Lewis the Fourteenth**, who began in 1643. He was then a child, but France was ruled by **Cardinal Mazarin**, as before by Cardinal Richelieu. By the **Peace of Westphalia** the two religions in Germany were put on a level, but the land was ruined, and from this time all power was in the hands of the princes. France got a great part of **Elsass**, which was cut off from the Empire. The kings of Sweden also got lands in Germany, but they became Princes of the Empire. From then between France and Spain the war went on till 1659, when France got Roussillon and some places in the Netherlands.

17. **European Colonies.**—Nearly all the seafaring powers of Europe made settlements in the newly-found lands in the east and in the west. Portugal began; then came Spain, and afterwards France, England, and the United Provinces. These settlements were of two kinds. Some, chiefly in Africa and the East Indies, were settlements for trade, which often grows into dominion, but where none stay

and leave their children behind them. Others, chiefly in America, were real colonies, which have grown into new English, Spanish, and Portuguese-speaking nations. But the colonies were not independent, like the old Greek colonies; they were all subject to the mother country. The Portuguese began their settlements in Africa before the Cape of Good Hope was found out. After that, they pressed further east, towards India and the Eastern Islands, and in the sixteenth century they had a greater eastern dominion than any other European power. But in America the Spaniards came first; for **Columbus**, who in 1492 reached the West India islands first, though a Genoese, was in the service of Ferdinand and Isabel. Others of the first discoverers, among them **Amerigo Vespucci**, from whom the continent took its name of **America**, were Italians in the service of foreign kings. Between 1519 and 1536 the great Spanish dominion in America was founded. In South America the Portuguese also made their great colony of Brazil. The French, English, and Dutch had chiefly to do with North America. The real beginning both of French and of English colonization began about the same time, in 1606 and 1607. The English colonies, of which **Virginia** came first, and then **New England**, have grown into the United States. There were also Dutch and Swedish colonies on those coasts, and France claimed a great territory to the north, south, and west. Thus a new European world arose beyond the Ocean. From this time the history of India, and still more that of America, becomes part of the history of Europe.

18. **Learning, Art, and Science.**—The movement in men's minds which led to the religious Reformation, led also to great advances in knowledge of all kinds. The **New Learning** spread itself from Italy over other lands. Latin still remained the language of learning and science, but men in most

lands began to write history and poetry in their own tongues. The religious disputes led to much writing on theological matters on all sides. The sixteenth century was also the age of the great Italian painters, and of many of the chief poets of England, Italy, Spain, and Portugal; France shone more in the way of prose. Different nations now knew more of each other's languages, the Italian language being specially studied. And, as the twelfth century had revived the study of the Roman Law in Italy, so now in the United Provinces arose the study of the **Law of Nations**, the rules by which nations hold themselves to be bound in matters of war and peace. Germany was kept back by its civil wars; but Luther's translation of the Bible fixed the standard of the German language, and ruled that High-Dutch should have the upperhand over Low. Men also got a greater knowledge of nature and truer notions of the movements of the heavenly bodies, though this new teaching was held by the Popes to be heretical. On the other hand, Pope Gregory the Thirteenth put the calendar right, which had never been put right since the time of Cæsar, and for a long time this reform was accepted by Catholics and refused by Protestants. By the Eastern Church it is refused still.

19. **Summary.**—During this time the relative importance of the powers of Europe changed greatly. The Empire practically came to an end; but the title of Emperor was still given to the German Kings of the House of Austria. The Spanish branch of that House rose to the first place in Europe; but, during the Thirty Years' War, France began to supplant it. The Italian states became dependencies of Spain, except so far as Venice still remained a bulwark against the Turks. Of the other bulwarks of Europe, Hungary had ceased to be an independent kingdom; the Turks held the greater part, and the Austrian Archdukes were Kings of the rest. Poland was at the

height of her power at the beginning of the period, but she went down towards the end. Meanwhile new powers were rising. England and Scotland, though still separate kingdoms, formed one state as regarded other nations. The revolt of the United Provinces from Spain had made a new nation. Sweden suddenly became one of the chief powers of Europe. Russia took the first steps towards greatness. The discovery of new lands in the east and west altogether changed the face of the world, and gave a new range for all the sea-faring powers. Meanwhile the changes in religion split the Churches of the West altogether asunder; but the same movement of men's minds which caused this caused also great advances of thought and knowledge in every way.

CHAPTER X.

THE GREATNESS OF FRANCE.

1. **Growth of the French Power.**—France now begins to take the place of Spain as the leading power in Europe. She had already humbled both branches of the House of Austria, and had dismembered the Empire itself. In 1661 **Lewis the Fourteenth** took the government into his own hands, and ruled more absolutely than any King before him. In 1665, on the death of Philip the Fourth of Spain, he claimed part of the Netherlands as belonging to his queen, though she had given up all such claims at her marriage. Down to 1679 he made various conquests in the Netherlands, and won the **County of Burgundy**, the city of **Besançon**, and some more towns in Elsass. He also attacked the United Provinces, which now began to help their old enemy Spain against their new enemy France.

The Emperor Leopold and some of the German princes also took part in the war. Lewis, who persecuted the Protestants in France, supported the Protestants of Hungary against the Emperor, and allied himself with the Turks, as Francis the First had done. In 1679, by the peace of **Nimwegen**, Lewis kept these conquests. But he still went on seizing places in Elsass, and in 1681 he seized **Strassburg** itself in time of peace. He also seized Avignon, and insulted the commonwealth of Genoa.

2. **England, the United Provinces, and France.**—But the power of Lewis was now checked by the union of England and the United Provinces. The Protector Cromwell, died in 1658, and, after a time of confusion, Charles the Second came back in 1660. Then England lost the position which she had held under Cromwell; for Charles truckled to France and took money from Lewis. There were wars between England and the United Provinces both under the Commonwealth and under Charles the Second. But meanwhile the **Princes of Orange** were for some generations **Stadholders** or chief magistrates of Holland, and one of them, William the Second, married a daughter of our Charles the First. His son **William**, who was also Stadholder after a while, was the leader in defending the Provinces against Lewis. He married his cousin Mary, daughter of **James Duke of York**, the brother of Charles the Second. In 1685 Charles died, and James, who had become a Roman Catholic, succeeded. His illegal doings caused him to be driven out in 1688, and **William and Mary** were chosen King and Queen. Thus England and the United Provinces were ready to withstand France together. Just at this time war broke out again over almost all Europe. King William, as the head of both countries, was the soul of the **Grand Alliance** which was formed to withstand France, and which took in the Emperor, the King of

Spain, and various German Princes. At last, in 1697, peace was made at **Ryswick,** by which Lewis gave up some other places which he had seized in Germany, but kept Strassburg. In 1702 King William died, and was succeeded by Anne, daughter of James the Second.

3. **War of the Spanish Succession.**—Under Charles the Second of Spain, who reigned from 1675 to 1700, that kingdom went down yet more than ever. As Charles had no children, there were disputes as to the succession, and several treaties were made to settle it. It was at last agreed that Spain should pass to the Emperor's son the Archduke Charles, and that the rest of the Spanish dominions in Europe should be divided. But when Charles of Spain died, he left all his dominions to **Philip Duke of Anjou,** a grandson of Lewis of France. Thus another war broke out, in which England, the United Provinces, the Empire, Brandenburg or Prussia, and Savoy, all took a part. The **Duke of Marlborough's** victories were now won, and England got **Gibraltar.** Peace was made in 1713 and 1714 by the treaties of **Utrecht** and **Rastadt.** Philip was acknowledged **King of Spain and the Indies**—that is of the settlements of Spain in America and the East; but Gibraltar and the island of Minorca were cut off from Spain, and kept by England. Charles, who in 1711 had succeeded to the Empire and to the Austrian states, took the Netherlands, Sardinia, the Kingdom of Naples, and part of the Duchy of Milan. The rest of that Duchy and the Kingdom of Sicily went to **Victor Amadeus,** Duke of Savoy. Before long, in 1715, Lewis the Fourteenth died. Though he had increased his dominions, his kingdom was greatly weakened by his wars, and above all by his persecution of the Protestants, which drove many of the most industrious people in the land to leave France and carry their skill elsewhere.

4. **Great Britain and Ireland.**—This was an E. Pr. H

important time as to the relations between the three kingdoms of England, Scotland, and Ireland. Scotland and Ireland had been conquered by Cromwell and made into one commonwealth with England. When Cnarles the Second came back, Scotland again became an independent kingdom, and Ireland became a dependency of England. The Scots were chiefly Presbyterians, that is, Protestants who had made greater changes than the Church of England had done, and they were much persecuted by Charles and James. So, when the English chose William and Mary, the Scots gladly chose them also, and thus secured their own religion. But the Irish were mainly Roman Catholics; so they clave to James, and King William had to conquer the land. Harsh laws were passed against the Roman Catholics, so that the Revolution, which brought freedom to England and Scotland, brought only bondage to Ireland. In Queen Anne's time, in 1707, England and Scotland were joined into the one Kingdom of **Great Britain**, on which Ireland remained dependent. As neither William nor Anne left children, the next Protestant heir, **George Elector of Hanover**, a descendant of James the First in the female line, was chosen to succeed, which he did on Anne's death in 1714.

5. **Germany and Hungary.**—The Emperor during most part of this time was **Leopold the First**, who reigned from 1658 to 1705. The German Princes now did much as they pleased, and some of them joined Lewis in his wars with the Empire. But the union of **Brandenburg** and **Prussia** had made a new German power, which grew greatly under Frederick William, who was called the **Great Elector**. In 1701 his son Frederick took the title of **King of Prussia**. The next king, Frederick William the First, greatly strengthened the Prussian army. Meanwhile, in 1683 the Turks besieged Vienna, but they were driven back by **John Sobieski** King of Poland and

Charles Duke of Lorraine. Hungary was now quite cleared of the Turks, and in 1687 the crown was made hereditary in the House of Austria. Under Leopold, under **Joseph**, who succeeded in 1705, and under **Charles the Sixth**, who reigned from 1711 to 1740, there were several Turkish wars till the peace of Passarowitz in 1718. Part of Servia, with the city of Belgrade, was now given up by the Turks.

6. **Italy.**—In Italy, the Duchy of **Savoy** and the Commonwealth of **Venice** are now the only states that have any history. The other states were changed about as foreign powers thought good, and by the Treaty of Utrecht the Emperor Charles the Sixth became almost as much master of Italy as Charles the Fifth had been. But Savoy was growing. Its Dukes took some part in every war, and gained something by every peace. Thus Duke **Victor Amadeus** gained by the Peace of Utrecht part of the Duchy of Milan and was made King of the island of Sicily. Meanwhile Venice still kept up the struggle with the Turks, though her power was sadly falling back. From 1645 to 1669 went on the **War of Candia**, so called from the long siege of the town of Candia in Crete. The island was now lost, but in 1684 the Venetians under **Francesco Morosini** conquered all Peloponnêsos, and kept it till 1715. The Turks then won back the peninsula, and from that time Venice kept none of her Greek dominions except the seven Ionian Islands and one or two points on the Albanian coast.

7. **Northern Europe.**—During the latter half of the seventeenth century Sweden still kept the place in Europe which had been won for her by Gustavus Adolphus. Besides her new possessions in Germany, the **Peace of Oliva** in 1660 gave her nearly all Livonia, and that part of Denmark which lay within the northern peninsula. In 1682 Sweden was made an absolute monarchy, as Denmark had been in 1660. Now in 1697 came the famous **Charles the Twelfth**, who

tried to do greater things than he was able to do. He was attacked by Denmark, Poland, and Russia all at once. Russia was now ruled by the famous **Peter the Great**, and Poland, after being cut short both by Sweden and Turkey, had risen again under her King **John Sobieski**. He was now dead, and the next King was Frederick Augustus, Elector of Saxony, called **Augustus the Strong**. Charles first beat the Danes, then the Russians in the Battle of **Narva**, then pressed on into Poland, and in 1704 drove out Augustus and caused the Poles to choose a new King, **Stanislaus Leszczynski**. But Charles was presently defeated by the Russians at Pultowa, and took shelter with the Turks. Thence he got back to his own dominions, and was at last killed in 1718, at Frederickshall in Norway. Under his sister Ulrica, peace was made, and Sweden now began to be cut short. Livonia and other lands were given up to Russia, and most of the German territory of Sweden was lost. The royal power too was made very small. From this time both Sweden and Poland ceased to be great powers.

8. **The Turks.**—Though the Turks still made some conquests, their power on the whole was going down on all sides. This was chiefly because they now left off the practice of levying a tribute of children on the subject nations, Greeks, Slaves, and others, which they had done ever since the time of Sultan Bajazet. The Turks took the strongest and cleverest children, and brought them up in their own religion. They became the chief servants of the Sultan, and of them was formed the force of the **Janissaries**, who were the great strength of the Turkish armies. Thus the strength of the subject nations was turned against themselves. But when the tribute was no longer levied, the Janissaries became a hereditary caste, and the Sultans had no longer such good soldiers and wise counsellors. Before long the subject nations began to think of making themselves free.

9. European Colonies and Settlements.— Meanwhile settlements beyond the ocean were being busily planted, especially by the great seafaring powers, England and the United Provinces. The English colonies in **North America** were now gradually planted, the last being Georgia in 1723, which made up the number of thirteen. But one of the chief of these, namely **New York**, was not an English colony from the beginning. It was at first a colony of the United Provinces, called **New Netherland**, with its capital **New Amsterdam**. But this was conquered by England in Charles the Second's time, and New Amsterdam was called New York, after James Duke of York, afterwards King James the Second. Whenever there was war between France and England, there was also war between their colonies in America. By the Peace of Utrecht in 1713, England got the French colony of Acadia, which was called **Nova Scotia**; but, shortly after this, the French founded **New Orleans** on the Mississippi. Meanwhile the English settlements in India had begun; but as yet the English were merely one set of traders along with the Portuguese, Dutch, French, and Danes. Some of these other settlements still survive, though the English have so greatly outstripped them. The **East India Company** began as a trading body under James the First; and trade gradually grew into dominion. By the end of the seventeenth century the English had made their three chief settlements of Calcutta, Bombay, and Madras. With the great islands to the east of India England had not much to do. The chief powers there were the Dutch and Spaniards.

10. **Summary.**—Thus during this time the power of Spain went down, till at last the great Spanish monarchy was altogether cut in pieces. France took the lead instead of Spain, and grew so fast, that it needed the union of several other powers to keep her in check. England began, under William the Third, to hold a

high place in all continental affairs. She also greatly extended her colonies in America, and began her dominion in India. The Empire had become a mere name; but the Emperors, as Austrian princes, had gained greatly in the Netherlands and Italy, and also as Kings of Hungary against the Turks. Another great German power was also growing up in the new kingdom of Prussia. Italy was dead, save that Savoy was advancing, and that Venice still gallantly withstood the Turks. The Turks, though they still made some conquests, were ceasing to be feared. Sweden and Poland sank from the rank of great powers. Russia meanwhile sprang up and grew at the expense of Sweden, Poland, and Turkey. In learning and literature France and England were at this time decidedly at the head.

CHAPTER XI.

THE ALLIANCE OF THE BOURBON KINGDOMS.

1. **France and Spain.**—The most lasting events of this time were the growth of Russia into a great power, and the rivalry between the House of Austria and the growing power of Prussia. Out of this last has come the present state of things in Germany. But what at the time specially distinguished this period was that, during the greater part of it, the Bourbon Kings of France and Spain were in close alliance with each other, and in constant rivalry with Great Britain. And, as that rivalry was mainly carried on among the colonies and distant possessions of those three powers, it led to great changes in distant parts —to the establishment of the great naval power of

England, to the foundation of the British dominion in India, and to the independence of the United States of America. But at the beginning of the time we have one war in which England and France were leagued against Spain; after that France and Spain were always leagued against England.

2. **The House of Austria.**—Meanwhile the centre of strictly European affairs is no longer indeed the Empire, but the Imperial House of Austria. For a while the rivalry between the **House of Austria** and the **House of Bourbon** still went on, only Spain was now Bourbon and not Austrian. The one war in which England and France were united was waged by **Cardinal Alberoni**, the minister of Philip the Fifth of Spain, to get back the Spanish possessions in Italy. But Spain got back nothing, only the Emperor and the King of Sicily exchanged their Italian kingdoms, so that the Emperor became **King of the Two Sicilies**, and the Duke of Savoy became **King of Sardinia** instead of Sicily. In the same year the Emperor Charles the Sixth, by an act called the **Pragmatic Sanction**, settled all his hereditary dominions on his daughter **Maria Theresa**; but by the **War of the Polish Election**, which began in 1733 between the Emperor and the two Bourbon kingdoms, the Austrian dominions in Italy were cut short. The Sicilies were given to a younger branch of the Spanish Bourbons, and Sardinia again got part of Milan. It was also settled that the Duchy of Lorraine should be given for life to Stanislaus, who had been King of Poland, and should, on his death, pass to France. Francis, Duke of Lorraine, who had married Maria Theresa, was to have Tuscany instead of his own duchy. Thus, by Lorraine becoming French, the Empire itself was cut short as well as the House of Austria, and the Austrian power, which had been so great at one part of Charles the Sixth's reign, went down a good deal before his death.

3. **Austria and Prussia.**—Charles the Sixth died in 1740, and his hereditary dominions, Hungary, Bohemia, Austria, etc., passed to his daughter Maria Theresa, who was called **Queen of Hungary**. No Emperor was chosen for two years, and meanwhile, **Charles Elector of Bavaria** claimed the whole Austrian dominions. **Silesia** was claimed and conquered by the new King of Prussia, Frederick the Second, called **Frederick the Great**; and in 1742 the Elector of Bavaria was chosen Emperor. England, Sardinia, and the United Provinces helped the Queen of Hungary, while France and Spain helped her enemies. In the end Frederick kept nearly all Silesia, Maria Theresa kept the rest of her hereditary dominions, and when the Emperor **Charles the Seventh** died in 1745, her husband Duke **Francis** was chosen Emperor. Maria Theresa, being herself Queen of Hungary and Bohemia, and being also the Emperor's wife, was called the **Empress-Queen**. Through her marraige both the Austrian dominions and the Empire passed into a new family, that of Lorraine. In 1756 the **Seven Years' War** began between the King of Prussia and the Empress-Queen. This time France was on the Austrian side, as were also Russia, Poland, and Sweden, while England helped Prussia. In this war Frederick, left thus almost alone, showed how great a general he was; but in 1762 Peter the Third of Russia changed sides and helped Frederick. In 1765, **Joseph**, the son of Francis and Maria Theresa, succeeded his father in the Empire, and ruled along with his mother in her hereditary dominions. After her death in 1780 he reigned alone. Joseph was a reformer, but he often did more harm than good by not showing respect to the old laws and customs of his kingdoms. He was succeeded in 1774 by **Leopold the Second**, and he in 1792 by the last Emperor, **Francis the Second**.

4. **Great Britain.**—Meanwhile Great Britain had

foreign kings, and was constantly mixed up with foreign wars. In some of these we had to withstand powers which wished to bring back the **Pretender**, the son of James the Second, instead of the two Kings George First and Second. Thus in 1715 Lewis the Fourteenth, just at the end of his reign, encouraged the Pretender to try to win the British crowns from King George. But this rebellion came to nothing. In the beginning of **Lewis the Fifteenth's** reign, when the **Duke of Orleans** was Regent and England was in alliance with France and the Emperor Charles against Spain, Spain and Charles the Twelfth of Sweden tried to bring in the Pretender. Again, in 1739, when George the Second was king, another war with Spain was forced by the people on the king and his minister **Sir Robert Walpole**. England also took a part in the war of the Austrian Succession and in the Seven Years' War. In these wars England and France were always on opposite sides. Then in 1745 **Charles Edward**, the son of the old Pretender, with French help, stirred up a rebellion as his father had done, but he was overthrown at Culloden. This war with France was chiefly waged by sea and in America, where many victories were won, and Canada was gained, under the administration of **William Pitt**, afterwards Earl of Chatham. After this, in the reign of George the Third, who succeeded in 1760, came the war in which the English colonies in **North America** became independent, and in 1782 **Ireland** became a kingdom independent of Great Britain, having its own parliament, though under the same king.

5. **France.**—After Lewis the Fourteenth came his great-grandson Lewis the Fifteenth, who also came to the crown as a child, and had a long reign, till 1774. In his time France extended her territory in two places. The Duchy of **Lorraine** fell to France at the death of Stanislaus in 1766. Thus with the Three Bishopricks and the French lands in Elsass, France had now

a compact territory taken from the Empire. France also at this time gained the Italian island of **Corsica**, which had belonged to Genoa. The Corsicans tried to make themselves free under the famous **Paoli**; but the Genoese in 1768 made over their rights to France; and the French conquered the island. All this while the state of France itself was getting worse and worse. But the storm did not burst in the days of Lewis the Fifteenth, but in those of the next king, his grandson **Lewis the Sixteenth**.

6. **Spain.**—From the reign of Philip the Fifth onward Spain greatly advanced at home and abroad, and it can hardly be doubted that her rise was owing to her having lost her dominion in Italy and become a compact national power. Portugal was but little heard of. In the latter part of the Seven Years' War, France and Spain together set upon Portugal as being an ally of England; but the Portuguese, with English help, drove them back.

7. **Italy.**—Italy was not now quite so downtrodden as in the time just before. The Italian principalities were indeed handed over from one prince to another, and the commonwealths now counted for nothing, save for one moment in 1746. Then Genoa rose and drove out an Austrian garrison, and we have seen that the Corsicans rose against Genoa. Still, except just after the Peace of Utrecht, Italy was not at this time so utterly under the power of one foreign king as it had been in the days of the Spanish dominion. In 1748, after many shiftings, the principalities of Italy were settled. Austria kept part of the Duchy of Milan. The King of Sardinia got another part, and, on the extinction of the House of the Medici, Francis of Lorraine, the Emperor **Francis the First**, got the Grand Duchy of Tuscany. In 1765 he was succeeded by his son Leopold who was afterwards Emperor, and who did much for the good of his duchy: and though Spain herself got no Italian territory,

a Spanish prince, Charles, who was afterwards King of Spain, got the kingdom of the Two Sicilies and another got the duchies of Parma and Piacenza. Thus there were four Bourbon princes reigning in Europe.

8. **The Netherlands.**—During this time the power of the United Provinces steadily went down, chiefly because their trade passed into the hands of Great Britain. In the Seven Years' War they supported the Queen of Hungary, and were therefore attacked by France. At this time, in 1747, the Princes of Orange were made **Hereditary Stadholders.** Towards the end of the period the commonwealth had become quite insignificant; and had fallen almost wholly under the control of Prussia. Meawhile in those provinces which had been Spanish and were Austrian, the changes made by the Emperor Joseph the Second towards the end of this time led to disturbances.

9. **Northern Europe.**—The Scandinavian kingdoms, especially Sweden, now became, like the United Provinces, of much less account than before. Sweden had wars with Russia, and in 1743 she had to give up the district of Carelia on the Gulf of Finland. After 1720 the government remained almost wholly aristocratic, till in 1772 the royal power was set up again. Meanwhile in Denmark the kings remained absolute, but the country flourished, and its naval power was strengthened. During this time too the Duchies of **Sleswick and Holstein** were united with the Danish crown, Holstein remaining a fief of the Empire, while Sleswick was not.

10. **The Growth of Russia.**—But the change which, above all others, marks this time, is the rise of Russia to be one of the great powers of Europe. This was mainly the work of **Peter the Great,** who reigned from 1682 to 1725. He made many reforms in his dominions, and greatly extended the Russian power. Russia had hitherto had no port but

Archangel on the White Sea, but in 1696 Peter won a haven on the Black Sea by taking **Azof** from the Turks. Next, the conquest of Livonia and the other lands which were given up by Sweden gave Russia a sea-board on the Baltic, where Peter founded his new capital of St. Petersburg. Thus Russia had now havens on three European seas, and Peter also increased his power on the Caspian, at the expense of Persia. He took the title of **Emperor of all the Russias**; which, besides giving offence to the German kings who still bore the title of Roman Emperors, amounted to a claim over all the Russian territory held by Poland. After Peter's time the power of Russia, with a few reverses, went on advancing. The crown did not follow any strict law of succession, but passed sometimes by will, sometimes by revolution, and it was often held by women. After Peter came his widow Catharine, and soon after his niece Anne, his daughter Elizabeth, and lastly **Catharine the Second**, who succeeded in 1762 on the murder of her husband, Peter the Third, and reigned till 1796. She greatly extended the Russian power at the expense of the Turks, and overthrew the last traces of the **Tartar** power by the conquest of the peninsula called **Crimea**, and the neighbouring lands on the Black Sea. This answers in the history of Russia to the conquest of Granada in the history of Spain.

11. **The Fall of Poland.**—Under Catharine the Second the power of Russia was also carried into the heart of Europe at the expense of Poland. All through the eighteenth century Poland grew weaker and weaker. Russia hindered all attempts at reform, and forced on the country the last two kings, **Augustus**, Elector of Saxony, son of Augustus the Strong, and **Stanislaus Poniatowski**, a native Pole. Then in 1772 Catharine joined with Frederick the Great and with the Empress-Queen, in her character as Queen of **Hungary**, to partition Poland, each taking some parts

which lay near to them. In 1793 Russia and Prussia each took another share, and in 1795 the kingdom of Poland was altogether destroyed, and what was left was divided among the three powers. Russia got back most of her old territory, and the chief part of Lithuania. Here the people mainly belonged to the Eastern Church, and had been often persecuted by Poland on account of their religion. Prussia took West Prussia, and so joined the kingdom of Prussia to her German territories. She also took the greater part of old Poland, and a small part of Lithuania. Austria or Hungary took the rest of old Poland, and some Russian territory. Thus Poland was wiped out of the map of Europe.

12. **The Turks.**—The Turks meanwhile ceased to be dreaded by Christian nations. Yet in the early part of the eighteenth century they were sometimes successful against Russia, and commonly so against Austria. Under Sultan **Mahmoud the First**, Belgrade, and all that had been lost by the Peace of Passarowitz, was won back by the **Peace of Belgrade** in 1739. But in the wars with Catharine the Second the Turks always lost. Thus by the **Peace of Kainardji**, in 1774, the Sultans gave up their superiority over the Khans of Crimea, which soon led to the conquest of that land by Russia. Russia too gained certain rights of interference in the principalities of **Moldavia** and **Wallachia,** which were dependent on Turkey. In 1792, by the **Peace of Jassy**, the Turkish frontier fell back to the Dniester. Moreover, since the Sultans ceased to levy the tribute of children, the subject nations grew stronger, and tried to revolt whenever they had a chance. In this they were always encouraged by Russia, though they seldom got any real help. All this is in some sort a falling back on much earlier times. Russia has again fleets on the Euxine threatening Constantinople, and the creed of the Eastern Church is no longer that of

merely subject or obscure nations, but that of one of the chief powers of Europe.

13. **The English power in India.**—During this time the trading settlements of the **East India Company** grew into the English dominion in India. The wars between England and France went on also in India. At one time **Dupleix**, the governor of Pondicherry, the chief French settlement in India, formed great schemes of Indian dominion for his own country. But in 1757 the English and their native allies under **Clive** utterly overthrew the French and their native allies in the **Battle of Plassy**. From that time England steadily advanced to the chief power in India. The other European settlements have been as nothing beside the dominion of England. The native states have been, one by one, incorporated with the British dominion or made dependent on it, just as Rome dealt with the lands round the Mediterranean. All this time the English dominion in India was not in the hands of the King's Government, but in that of the Company. But in 1784, a body called the **Board of Control** was founded, to control the Company in certain cases by the King's authority. After Clive, the most famous name in Indian History is that of the Governor-General **Warren Hastings**. He was impeached—that is, accused by the House of Commons before the House of Lords—of misdoings of various kinds; but, after a trial of many years, he was acquitted.

14. **The Independence of the United States.** —During this time the English colonies in North America grew into a separate English-speaking nation. In all the wars among the European powers, their colonies in America joined; and the wars which England had with France and Spain in America led to great results. The thirteen English colonies lay along the east coast, and were hemmed in by the French colonies of **Canada** and

Louisiana to the north and west, and the Spanish colony of **Florida** to the south. In 1759, Canada was conquered by the English, and it has since been an English colony. Then, by the treaty of 1763, Florida was given up to England, and Louisiana was divided between England and Spain; thus France was quite shut out of North America. Then the British Government tried to tax the thirteen colonies, on which they revolted, and were helped, first by France, and afterwards by Spain. In 1776, the colonies declared themselves independent, each colony forming an independent state, joined together by a lax Confederation. In 1783 Great Britain acknowledged the independence of the thirteen colonies as the **United States of America.** Florida was given back to Spain, but Great Britain kept Canada, with the colonies of New Brunswick, Nova Scotia, and Newfoundland. Thus the United States were hemmed in to the north and south, but they grew to the west, where many new states were soon added. In 1789 the States made their confederation much closer under the new constitution. The first President was **George Washington,** who had been the great leader of the colonists during the War of Independence.

15. **Summary.**—This time then was one of great changes, especially in distant parts of the world. In Europe itself there was no very great change, except the wiping out of Poland. Great Britain, France, and Spain all kept much the same European position. Prussia had risen to greatness; but this was not the growth of a new nation: it was only that the chief power in Germany began to pass to a particular German state. Sweden and the United Provinces sank from a position which was really too great for their strength. But the mere extent of their territory was not greatly altered. The really great events of this time were the growth of Russia in Eastern Europe,

the establishment of the British power in India, and the foundation of the United States in America. The rise of Russia brought into importance both the Russian nation, and also the Eastern Church, which had been in the back-ground ever since the fall of the Eastern Empire. And this gave a great stir to those nations akin to Russia by race or religion which were in bondage to the Turks. But the change in America and India was still greater. The English-speaking people, both in Europe and in America, were marked out as the leaders in colonization and distant dominion. No power ever before held so great a distant dominion. as distinguished from a real colony, as the British dominion in India. For the provinces of old Rome all lay together, and the Spanish possessions in America were strictly colonies. This time too was one of great advance in physical and moral science and in mechanical discovery. Men's minds also were more astir on questions of religion, government, and society than they had ever been before. Everything was making ready for the greatest changes which Europe had seen for many ages.

CHAPTER XII.

THE FRENCH REVOLUTION.

1. **The French Republic.**— We have now come to times which a few old people can still remember. France is now the centre of everything, and men in France were now bent upon changing everything, good and bad. The great **French Revolution** began when Lewis the Sixteenth called together the **States-General** in 1789, which had not met since 1614; all that time the kings had never consulted the representatives of the nation. So, when the States

came together, they began to make the greatest changes in everything, sweeping away the absolute power of the king and the privileges of the nobles and clergy, dividing the land into departments instead of the old provinces which had once been separate states, and annexing Avignon and Venaissin, and the little that was left of Elsass. A new constitution left the King very little power, and restored the old title of **King of the French**. In 1792 kingship was abolished, and the power was vested in a **National Convention**. In 1793 the King was beheaded, and then followed the **Reign of Terror**, in which one party after another beheaded its enemies In 1795 began a time of somewhat more quiet under the **Directory**; but in 1799 they too were upset by **Napoleon Buonaparte**. He was by birth an Italian of Corsica, and counted as a Frenchman only because of the late French conquest of that island. He now took the government into his own hands by the title of **Consul**, and in 1804, when his power was fully established, he called himself **Emperor of the French**. Thus all these changes only ended in a new despotism.

2. **The Wars of the Revolution.**—Meanwhile the new commonwealth was fighting with most of the powers of Europe. Before Lewis the Sixteenth was beheaded, war began with the Emperor and the King of Prussia, and war with England followed directly after. From this time till 1815 there was no real peace, though there were many stoppages, and though the powers engaged often changed sides. Some lands were altogether annexed to France; others were made into separate commonwealths, which were really French dependencies. The first part of the war lasted till 1797: It was carried on in the Netherlands, along the Rhine, and in Italy. It was in these Italian campaigns that Napoleon Buonaparte first began to be famous. In this war France got the Austrian

E. Pr. I

Netherlands from the Emperor Francis, and also Savoy and Piedmont. And when peace was made, the Emperor and the French Republic, like Maximilian and Lewis the Twelfth, agreed to divide the territories of Venice between them. So the old commonwealth came to an end. Venice and Dalmatia became Austrian, and France took the Ionian Islands. Then came a war in Egypt, and, in 1790, an attack on Switzerland, which henceforth counted as a French dependency. Then in 1799 came another war with the Empire and with Russia. In 1801 Buonaparte, as Consul, made peace with the Empire, by which all Germany west of the Rhine was yielded to France. In 1802 he made peace with England at **Amiens**, but war broke out again almost directly.

3. **The Reign of Napoleon Buonaparte.**—All men's old ideas had now so utterly died away that Buonaparte ventured to give himself out as the successor of Charles the Great. He crowned himself as Emperor at Paris in 1804, and in the next year he made part of Northern Italy into a kingdom and was crowned **King of Italy** at Milan. He was now again at war with England, and England never again made peace with him till his fall. In 1805 his naval power was broken at the **Battle of Trafalgar**; but in his land campaigns from 1805 to 1811 he brought nearly all Western Europe under his power. He set up his brothers as Kings, and moved them from one kingdom to another. When his power was at the highest, the **French Empire**, as it was called, and his kingdom of Italy, took in all Germany west of the Rhine, all the Netherlands, a great part of North-Western Germany, most part of Italy and a large territory beyond the Hadriatic. His brother-in-law **Murat** was King of Naples, and his brother **Joseph** King of Spain, and most of the German princes had become his dependents. In 1812 he attacked Russia, but he came back the next year,

having gained nothing. Then in 1813 the whole German people rose against him, and Germany was set free in the **Battle of Leipzig**. Meanwhile the English, under the **Duke of Wellington**, had been freeing Spain and Portugal from Joseph Buonaparte. So in 1814 the allies entered France on both sides; Buonaparte abdicated, but was allowed to keep the little island of Elba. **Lewis the Eighteenth**, a brother of Lewis the Sixteenth, became King of France, but in the next year 1815, Buonaparte came back. He was now utterly overthrown by the English and Prussians at **Waterloo**, and he was kept in ward for the rest of his days in the little island of St. Helena. By the **Treaties of Paris and Vienna**, France gave up her conquests, and kept nearly the same boundaries as she had before the Revolution began.

4. **The Fall of the Empire.**—Next to France itself no part of Europe changed more during these times than Germany. The Roman Empire and the German Kingdom were now formally wiped out. When Buonaparte began to call himself Emperor of the French, the Emperor Francis called himself **Hereditary Emperor of Austria**, so utterly had the old meaning of the title been forgotten. In 1805 Buonaparte defeated the Austrians and Russians in the **Battle of Austerlitz**, and then many of the German princes joined him. They threw off their allegiance to the Empire, and made themselves into the **Confederation of the Rhine**, of which Buonaparte was called the **Protector**. Three of them, the Electors of **Bavaria** and **Saxony** and the Duke of **Württemberg**, called themselves Kings. In the same year 1806, the Emperor Francis formally resigned the Empire, and no Roman Emperor has been chosen since. But he went on reigning in his hereditary dominions, calling himself Emperor of Austria. In the same year Prussia was overthrown in the **Battle of Jena**. Her German dominions were cut

short, and the more part of her Polish dominions were made into a **Grand Duchy of Warsaw**, which was given to the new King of Saxony. Then in 1809 Austria was again overthrown at **Wagram**, and lost all her south-western dominions. Thus, by 1811, all Germany, except the parts left to Austria and Prussia, was either joined on to France or was wholly under Buonaparte's power. Then came the great deliverance of 1813. The people rose first, and the princes had to follow. After Buonaparte's fall the princes and free cities of Germany joined together into a lax **Confederation**, the presidency of which was given to Austria. Of this Confederation, the Sovereigns of Austria, Prussia, Denmark, Great Britain, and the new Kingdom of the Netherlands, were members for those parts of their dominions which lay within Germany. That is to say, in the case of our own King, for **Hanover**, which was now called a kingdom.

5. **Italy.**—Meanwhile the states of Italy were changed backwards and forwards. Parts were annexed to France, other parts were made, first into dependent commonwealths, and afterwards, in Buonaparte's time, into dependent principalities. But, when Buonaparte's power was at its height, the whole peninsula was, in one way or another, really in his hands. The Pope, **Pius the Seventh**, he had carried away into France. But Sicily and Sardinia were kept by their own Kings: for they were islands, and the English fleet took care of them. After the fall of Buonaparte, the Pope, the Kings of Sardinia and the Two Sicilies, and some of the other princes got their dominions again. But the commonwealths were not set up again; only little **San Marino** was allowed to remain. Genoa was joined to Piedmont; and the Duchy of Milan and the Venetian possessions were again given to Austria, by the name of the **Kingdom of Lombardy and Venice**. Thus all Italy was parted out among despotic princes, over whom Austria had again the chief

power. It was only in the Sardinian states that the dynasty, though still despotic, was at least national.

6. **Spain and Portugal.**—In the reign of **Charles the Third**, who had been King of the Two Sicilies, Spain greatly looked up again. Under **Charles the Fourth**, when the French Revolution began, Spain had first acted against France, but she afterwards changed sides and joined France against England and Portugal, and the Spanish fleet was overthrown along with the French at Trafalgar. Yet Buonaparte made the King abdicate; he then in 1807 got the king's son Ferdinand into his own power, and made his own brother Joseph King. But the patriotic Spaniards were helped by the English, and Spain was delivered. In 1814 Ferdinand came back; but he overthrew the constitution which had been made while he was away. Meanwhile Portugal too was overrun by the French. The King **John the Sixth** went over to Brazil and reigned there, whilst the Portuguese at home joined the English and Spaniards in the war of independence.

7. **The Netherlands.**—Those provinces of the Netherlands which had been held, first by Spain and then by Austria, were added to France early in the Revolutionary war. Then in 1795 the United Provinces became a republic dependent on France. Afterwards they were made into a kingdom for Buonaparte's brother **Lewis,** and at last they were joined to France. At the Peace, both the United Provinces and the Austrian Netherlands were made into a single **Kingdom of the Netherlands,** under **William, Prince of Orange,** who was also a member of the German Confederation as Grand Duke of Luxemburg.

8. **Switzerland.** — The old League of the Thirteen Cantons, with their allied and subject states, went on till the French came in 1798. Their coming set **Vaud** and other subject districts

free, but they had as little respect for the old democracies as they had for Kings or oligarchies. They made the whole League into what they called the **Helvetic Republic**; this was no longer a Confederation of independent states, but the cantons were mere departments, **Geneva** and some other of the allied states were added to France, some now, some afterwards. The new system did not suit the Swiss; and in 1803, by the **Act of Mediation**, Buonaparte gave them a Federal Constitution again. Several of the allies and subjects now became cantons. At the Peace the **Swiss Confederation** of twenty-two States was made, but the tie among them was very lax. Geneva and some other districts which had been joined to France now became separate cantons.

9. **Great Britain and Ireland.**—England was at war with France during the whole of the wars which followed the French Revolution, save only the short stoppage which followed the **Peace of Amiens**. The victories of **Lord Nelson** broke the power of France by sea, and the land campaigns of the **Duke of Wellington** freed Spain and Portugal. In 1798 there was a rebellion in Ireland, and in 1800 Ireland was joined with Great Britain into the one **United Kingdom of Great Britain and Ireland**. Our Kings now dropped the title of **King of France**, which they had kept ever since the Treaty of Troyes. The European possessions of England were not greatly changed at the Peace. The islands of **Malta** in the Mediterranean and of **Heligoland** in the German Ocean became British possessions. And the **Ionian Islands** were made into a commonwealth under British protection. In the distant parts of the world England made the greatest advances. During the administration of the **Marquess Cornwallis** and the **Marquess Wellesley**, the greater part of India was either annexed to the British dominion or brought under British influence. Colonization too

began in **Australia**. And in the course of the war large conquests were made among the colonies of France, Spain, and Holland. England thus got **Ceylon** and several other islands, the **Cape of Good Hope** in South Africa and a small territory in South America. During the last years of the French war, from 1813 to 1815; a war unhappily arose between England and the United States, but it ended without any change in the possessions of either.

10. **The Scandinavian Kingdoms.**—This was a time of great changes in the three kingdoms of Denmark, Sweden, and Norway. At the beginning of the French Revolution, the King of Sweden was **Gustavus the Third**, who restored the royal power; but he was murdered in 1792. His successor **Gustavus the Fourth** was deposed in 1809, and the old freer constitution was restored. Both these Kings had wars with Russia, and in the time of Gustavus the Fourth, Sweden lost all **Finland**. The new King **Charles the Thirteenth** had no children; so the Swedes chose **Bernadotte**, one of Buonaparte's generals, to be Crown Prince or heir to the throne, and to succeed when the King died. In 1813, Sweden, in virtue of her German possessions, joined in the war of liberation in Germany; so Bernadotte fought against his old master. But Denmark had been on the side of France; so at the peace it was settled that **Norway** should be taken from Denmark, and added to Sweden to make up for the loss of Finland. But the Norwegians refused to be joined on to Sweden; they made themselves a very free constitution, and chose a Danish prince for their King. They had to submit so far as to agree that Sweden and Norway should always have the same King; but Norway remained a distinct kingdom with its own constitution. At the same time Swedish **Pomerania** was given to Denmark, and afterwards exchanged with Prussia for **Lauenburg**.

Thus Sweden was cut off altogether from the East and South coast of the Baltic; but the whole of the Scandinavian peninsula was joined under one sovereign.

11. **Russia and Poland.**—After Catharine the Second came her son **Paul**, who was mad and was killed in 1801. He for a while joined Austria in the war with France, but afterwards made a separate peace. His son **Alexander** was at peace with France till 1805, when he joined with Austria against Buonaparte. But, after the French victories over Austria and Prussia, he and Buonaparte made a treaty at **Tilsit**, and for six years Russia and France were at peace. During this time Russia won Finland from Sweden; and in a war with Turkey she advanced her frontier to the Danube, and also won a large territory from Persia. Then in 1813 came the French invasion of Russia, and after that Russia took a chief part in putting down Buonaparte. At the Peace the Grand Duchy of Warsaw, which had been increased by part of the Austrian dominions in Poland, was made into a **Kingdom of Poland** with a constitution of its own, which was joined to Russia as a separate kingdom, like Sweden and Norway. Only **Posen** was given back to Prussia. Alexander of Russia now called himself **Emperor of all the Russias and King of Poland**. **Cracow** also, the ancient capital of Poland, was made a free city under the protection of Russia, Prussia, and Austria.

12. **The Turks.**—Under the Sultans, **Selim the Third**, who began in 1789, and was deposed in 1807, and **Mahmoud the Second**, whose reign went on till 1839, the Ottoman power had to struggle with many enemies. Besides the wars, first with France and then with Russia, the subject nations, both Christian and Mahometan, were trying to become independent. The great **Pashas** or governors of the distant provinces tried to set up for themselves, just like the

state of things at the breaking up of the Caliphate. In Albania both the Christians of **Souli** and the Mahometan **Ali Pasha** withstood the Turkish power; and, to the north of them, the Christians of **Cernagora** or **Montenegro** had never been conquered at all. Northward again, **Servia** revolted, and, when it was conquered, it revolted again, till it became, as it still is, a separate state under the Sultan's superiority. In Egypt too the **Mamelukes** had become practically independent. It was the policy of Russia to stir up discontent among all the subject nations, especially among those which belonged to the Eastern Church.

13. **America.**—The new constitution of the **United States** came into force in the same year in which the French Revolution began. Both Washington and several Presidents after him were very able rulers. Many states were added to the Union in the west, and in 1803 the United States bought the territory of **Louisiana**, which Spain had again given back to France. Slavery was abolished in all the Northern States, and almost the only check to the advance of the Union was the two years' war with England. Meanwhile, when Spain was overrun by the French, the Spanish colonies in America began to set up for themselves, as the English colonies had done. **Mexico** and **Chili** both revolted in 1810. Mexico was recovered for a while, but it revolted again in 1820, as **Peru** did also. Also in the Island of **Hayti** or Saint Domingo, in the West Indies, which, at the beginning of the Revolution, belonged partly to France and partly to Spain, the negroes in both parts of the island set up for themselves. There have been many revolutions in all these countries, and for a while both in Hayti and in Mexico men of different colours called themselves Emperors, as Buonaparte did in France. But, in the end, all the Spanish American states but Brazil became commonwealths.

14. **Summary.**—Thus, in less than one generation, Europe was more changed than it had ever been before in so short a time. Nowhere had all old ideas, both good and bad, been so thoroughly cast away as they now were in France and wherever France had influence. But, though much good perished with the bad, and though France has never had a lasting government since, yet the change was on the whole for good. In no part of Europe has there been since that time so much corruption and oppression as there was in many parts before. The wars of those times also paved the way for the events of our own day, especially for the union of Germany and Italy into great nations. France at the end of the war came out with her old boundaries and with a king of the old dynasty; but her whole social and political state was utterly changed. In Germany the Empire had changed into a lax confederation, in which the two great states of Prussia and Austria were sure to be rivals. Spain and Portugal had got back their old dynasties. Italy was still cut up into small states, chiefly under the influence of Austria. In Switzerland the old distinctions had been wiped out, and the whole land had become an equal confederation. The Netherlands had been joined into a single kingdom. The Scandinavian kingdoms had been quite changed by Sweden losing her possessions in Finland and Germany, and by Norway, which had so long been joined with Denmark, having the same King as Sweden. Russia had grown at every point, and Poland had been set up again as a separate, though not an independent, kingdom. The power of the Ottoman Turks was weakened in every way, and the Christian nations under their yoke were striving for, and some of them winning, their independence.

CHAPTER XIII.

THE REUNION OF GERMANY AND ITALY.

1. **Character of the Time.**—We have now come to our own times, times which have been as full of great events as any times before them. What most distinguishes the changes of our own day has been that most of them have been brought about through the feeling of **nationality**—that is, through the wish of men who speak the same tongue, and feel that they belong to the same nation, to come together under one government. This has been shown, above all things, by the joining together of the German and Italian nations, after each of them had been so long split up into many small states. A long peace has been followed by many wars, and those wars have been carried on with much greater armies, and finished in a much shorter time, than the wars of earlier times. In our times France has not been the centre of everything in the way in which it was during the wars which followed the French Revolution; still we cannot understand what went on anywhere else without knowing what was going on in France at the same time. So our account of the last sixty years will best begin with a sketch of the later revolutions of France.

2. **The Revolutions of France.**—After the final overthrow of Buonaparte, Lewis the Eighteenth came back and reigned as a constitutional king, though many people about him wished to have the old state of things back again. Then came his brother **Charles the Tenth**, the last King who was crowned at Rheims and called himself **King of France**. In July 1830 he put forth some proclamations which were

wholly against the law; so he was driven out, and his kinsman **Louis-Philippe** Duke of Orleans was made king with the title of **King of the French,** and a freer constitution. In his time, **Louis-Napoleon Buonaparte,** a nephew of the former Buonaparte, twice tried to disturb the King's government. The first time he was let go free; the second time he was imprisoned, but escaped. In February 1848 Louis-Philippe himself was driven out, and a Republic was set up. In June of the same year, a revolt of the extreme Republicans was put down by General **Cavaignac.** For this service many people wished to make him the first President of the new commonwealth, like Washington in the United States. But meanwhile Louis-Napoleon Buonaparte had been allowed to come back, and, when the time of voting came, he was chosen by many votes over Cavaignac. He was to be President for four years, and he swore to be faithful to the commonwealth. But in December 1851 he rose up against the commonwealth, dissolved the Assembly by force, caused many men to be slain in the streets, and imprisoned and banished many others. Then he called himself President of the Republic for ten years, and in December 1852 he called himself **Emperor of the French,** like his uncle.

3. **The Wars of France.**—Both during the reigns of the three Kings and under the Republic, France had no great wars. She put down the pirate state of **Algiers,** and made that part of Africa into a French colony. And, when Rome became a republic as well as France, French troops were sent to put the Roman Republic down. When Louis-Napoleon Buonaparte first called himself Emperor, he said that the Empire should be peace. But in his time France was at war with the three chief powers of the continent, one after another. In 1854, when there was a quarrel between Russia and Turkey,

France made war on **Russia** together with England. In 1859, when there was a quarrel between Austria and Sardinia, France made war on **Austria**. When peace was made, **Nizza** and **Savoy**, the last remains of the Burgundian possessions of the King of Sardinia, were given to France. Lastly in 1870, when there was talk of a distant kinsman of the King of Prussia being made King of Spain, France made war on **Prussia**, and the French troops crossed the German frontier. But all Germany fought for Prussia. The German troops entered France, won many battles, besieged and took Paris, and, when peace was made, France had to give back the German land of Elsass and part of Lorraine, so that the French frontier no longer reaches to the Rhine. By this time France was again a commonwealth. For early in the war Buonaparte was taken prisoner, and, when this was known in Paris, he was deposed, and a Republic proclaimed. **M. Thiers**, who had been minister under Louis-Philippe, was soon after chosen President of the Republic, and peace was made with Germany. Soon after this Paris was held by the **Communists** or extreme republicans, and had to be besieged and taken again. Since then, M. Thiers has resigned, and in 1874, **Marshal MacMahon** was made President for seven years.

4. **The Union of Germany.**—After the German Confederation was set up in 1815, though most of the princes forgot their promises to their subjects, yet things on the whole tended towards union. In 1818 Prussia began the **Zollverein** or **Customs Union**, which was gradually joined by most of the German states. Its members levied no duties on merchandize passing from one to another, but only at the common frontier. In 1848 there were revolutions in Prussia, Austria, and other German states, and a fruitless attempt was made to join Germany more closely together under an Emperor and a common

Parliament. In 1866 a war broke out between Prussia and Austria, in which the German states took different sides. Prussia speedily got the better, and, by the peace, the German Confederation came to an end. Austria was altogether shut out from Germany. Hanover and some other states were annexed to Prussia, and the other northern states were formed into the **North-German Confederation**, under the presidency of Prussia. During the war with France the southern states also joined the Confederation. And, while the siege of Paris was going on, **King William** of Prussia received the title of **German Emperor** from the German princes and free cities. Thus, as the German lands held by France were given back, all Germany, except Austria and the other German possessions of the Austrian house, is now more closely joined together than it had ever been since the great Interregnum. Each state of the Empire keeps its own government and assembly, and there is the Emperor and Assembly of all Germany over all.

5. **The Union of Italy.**—From 1815 to 1848 there were some conspiracies and insurrections in Italy, but the land was kept down under the power of Austria and the princes supported by Austria. In the Sardinian states only, where **Charles Albert** began to reign in 1831, there was, though not as yet freedom, yet national spirit. In 1846 the present Pope **Pius the Ninth** began to reign, and at first favoured reform and freedom. Then in 1848 most parts of Italy rose. **Sicily** chose a King separate from Naples; Rome and Venice became commonwealths; Milan also rose against Austria. Charles Albert made war against Austria, but he was defeated at **Novara** in 1849 and abdicated. The Pope and the other princes now came back, and freedom was everywhere put down by the Austrians and French. Only in the Sardinian states **Victor Emmanuel** reigned as a constitu-

tional King. In 1859 war arose between him and Austria, in which Sardinia was helped by France. Buonaparte promised to free Italy from the Alps to the Hadriatic; but, though the Austrians were beaten and had to give up Lombardy, they were allowed to keep Venetia. Now too Savoy and Nizza were taken by France. Then the two Sicilies were delivered by **Garibaldi**, and joined to the kingdom of Victor Emmanuel, to which all the other Italian states joined themselves wherever they could. Only at Rome the French still kept the Pope in power. Thus in 1861 Victor Emmanuel was made **King of Italy.** Then in 1866, when Prussia and Austria were at war, Italy joined Prussia, and Austria had to give up Venetia. Lastly in 1870, when the French were at war with Germany, they could no longer keep their troops at Rome; so Rome too became free, and is now the capital of Italy. Thus the House of Savoy has lost all its dominions beyond the Alps, but has gained the Kingdom of all Italy.

6. **Hungary, Austria, and Poland.**—After the peace, **Francis the First** of Hungary, who had been the last Emperor **Francis the Second**, went on reigning in Hungary, Austria, and his other dominions, including the Austrian part of Poland, till his death in 1836, when he was succeeded by **Ferdinand the Fifth.** Meanwhile **Alexander** reigned over Russia and the new kingdom of Poland, till his death in 1825, when he was succeeded by **Nicholas.** The union of Russia and Poland did not answer. The Polish constitution was often broken; so in 1831 the Poles revolted, but the revolt was put down, and their constitution was taken away. In 1863 the Poles revolted again against the present Russian Emperor **Alexander the Second.** And when this revolt was put down, the Polish kingdom was quite swept away. Between the two revolts, in 1846, the commonwealth of **Cracow** was annexed to Austria.

Thus all traces of Polish freedom have been swept away. But in the neighbouring land of Hungary the old freedom has been won back again. In 1847 and 1848, there were revolutions in Hungary and Austria. Ferdinand abdicated and was succeeded in Austria by **Francis Joseph**; but the Hungarians would not acknowledge the abdication, which was not made after their laws, and after a while they set up a commonwealth. Hungary was then conquered by Austria with the help of Russia, and it remained crushed till the war between Austria and Prussia. Then Hungary and Austria were joined as separate states under a common sovereign, and Francis Joseph was lawfully crowned **King of Hungary** in 1867. Since then Hungary and Austria have agreed well together; but there have been discontents among some of the other nations which also form part of the dominions of the Austrian House.

7. Spain and Portugal.—After Ferdinand the Seventh of Spain came back, there were several risings, because the new constitution was not kept. At last, in 1822, it was altogether set aside by the help of French troops. When Ferdinand died in 1833, a civil war went on till 1840 between the partisans of his daughter **Isabel** and those of his brother **Charles** or **Don Carlos**, who was favoured by the Basque lands in the north. There were several other disturbances and insurrections, but Isabel reigned till she was driven out in 1868. In 1870 **Amadeus**, son of the King of Italy, was chosen king. In 1873 he abdicated, and a republic was set up, but much confusion followed. In 1875 the son of Isabel was called back as **Alfonso the Twelfth**, and meanwhile another Don Carlos, a grandson of the old one, has been carrying on a civil war in the Basque lands. Besides all this, Spain has also had disputes with the one great colony which she has left, namely, the island of **Cuba**. In Portugal also there was for a while much confusion and civil wars. After the Peace, John the Sixth, **King of Portugal and Brazil**, stayed for some years in Brazil, the only time that an European state has been governed from the New World. In 1822 Brazil separated from Portugal, but, unlike all other American states, it became a constitutional monarchy under the King's son, **Don Pedro** or Peter. He reigned in Brazil as **Emperor**, and, when he succeeded to the crown of Portugal, he gave up both crowns, that of Portugal to his daughter **Maria**, and that of Brazil to his son **Pedro**. Since then the two crowns have been separate, and Brazil has gone on better than any other South-American state. In Portugal there was a civil war for a while between Don Pedro, as Regent for his daughter **Maria**, and his younger brother **Don Miguel** or **Michael**, who reigned from 1828 to 1832. Then Maria was acknowledged. Since then, under Queen Maria and her son the present King Lewis, there have been some disputes and risings, but no serious change.

8. **The Netherlands.**—The union of all the Netherlands into a single kingdom did not answer. For the northern parts, which had been the United Provinces, and the southern, which had been, first the Spanish, and then the Austrian, Netherlands, differed in religion, and to some extent in language. In 1830, the southern provinces revolted, and the kingdom was divided. The House of Orange went on reigning in the north as **Kings of the Netherlands**, while the south became the **Kingdom of Belgium**. Its first king was **Leopold** of Saxe-Coburg, whose son of the same name is the present king. Since then both kingdoms have been constitutionally governed. There have been disputes about the Duchy of **Luxemburg**, which was held by the King of the Netherlands as a member of the German Confederation, and Luxemburg has been declared neutral.

9. **Switzerland.**—Since 1815 the boundaries of

E. P.r   K

Switzerland have not changed, nor has the Confederation been at war with any other state; but there have been great internal changes. In 1831 there were disputes in many of the cantons, which ended in their governments being made more popular. In 1847 there was even a civil war between the Catholic and Protestant cantons. In the next year 1848 the tie between the cantons was made much closer by a new **Federal Constitution**, which is in many things like that of the United States, only, instead of a single President, there is a Council of Seven with much smaller powers. In 1874 this constitution was again revised; the powers of the cantons were again lessened, and those of the Federal body increased.

10. **The Scandinavian Kingdoms.**—In Sweden and Norway there has been no revolution or great change of any kind since the Peace. The kings of the **House of Bernadotte** have reigned over both kingdoms, each keeping its own separate constitution. In Sweden of late years the constitution has been improved, and more religious liberty given. But in Denmark this has been a time of great changes. The kings remained absolute till 1848, when **Frederick the Seventh**, on coming to the crown, at once gave his people a free constitution. But disputes arose between the Kingdom of Denmark and the two Duchies, **Holstein**, which is wholly German, and which was a member of the German Confederation, and **Sleswick**, which was not a member of the Confederation, and where the people are German in the south and Danish in the north. There was fighting about this till 1851, but then Denmark kept both Duchies. In 1864, under the present King **Christian the Ninth**, there was another war, after which the Duchies were given up to Prussia and Austria together. Since the war between Prussia and Austria in 1866, they have been kept by Prussia only. The northern part of Sleswick was to have been given back to

Denmark, but this has not been done. In 1874 a constitution was given to **Iceland**, which forms part of the Danish dominions.

11. **Russia, Turkey, and Greece.**—During this time there have still been wars between Russia and Turkey, and several parts of the Turkish dominions have been cut off. In 1821 the Greeks revolted in most parts of the Turkish dominions, and in Greece itself the Greek and Albanian inhabitants, with a little help from the other subject nations and much more from volunteers from Western Europe, were able to hold their ground against the Turks. But in 1827, Sultan **Mahmoud** asked help of **Mahomet Ali**, the Pasha of Egypt, who had made himself nearly independent, and between them the Greeks might have been altogether crushed, had not England, France, and Russia, stepped in and destroyed the Turkish fleet at Pylos or **Navarino** in 1827. Then the French drove out the Egyptians, and Greece became free. The first King, **Otho of Bavaria**, was turned out in 1862, and was succeeded by **George of Denmark**; and in 1864 the **Ionian Islands** were added to the kingdom. Meanwhile there was war between Russia and Turkey in 1828, by which some further advantages were gained by Russia. Then came wars with Mahomet Ali of Egypt, which ended in 1841 by Egypt becoming practically independent. Then in 1854 another war began between Russia and Turkey, in which England, France, and Sardinia, gave help to the Turks. By the Peace in 1856, the Russian frontier was moved away from the Danube, as the frontier of France has since been moved away from the Rhine. The **Rouman** principalities, Moldavia and Wallachia, have been made into a principality which is practically independent. In 1875 the Christians in the Turkish provinces of Bosnia and Herzegovina revolted, and war is still going on there. Meanwhile Russia has made great

advances in different parts of Asia, and the present Emperor Alexander has made a great reform at home by setting free the serfs.

12. **Great Britain and Ireland.**—Our own history during this time consists chiefly of reforms at home, and of both warfare and colonization in distant parts. We have had no great European warfare, except the war with Russia in 1854. All Great Britain has long been firmly knit together. But in Ireland, notwithstanding all efforts to put Ireland and Great Britain on a level, the remembrance of old wrongs still keeps up a spirit of disaffection. The British colonies have vastly extended themselves in North America, South Africa, and above all in **Australia**, and most of these have received constitutions which make them nearly independent in their internal affairs. In 1837 there was a revolt of the French Canadians; but since then **Canada** has been highly prosperous, and has been joined with some of the other North-American colonies into a single Federal body. The slave-trade in our colonies was forbidden in 1807, and slavery itself was abolished in 1833. In India the British power has greatly advanced, and several provinces have been annexed. In 1858 the native soldiers mutinied, and, after the mutiny was quelled, the government of India was taken from the Company and given to the Crown; so that the Queen is now direct sovereign of India. And the great extent of our colonies and distant possessions has led us into several wars in various parts of the world, as with **China, Persia, Abyssinia,** and the **Ashantees** in Africa. Thus, throughout this time, Great Britain has been more and more taking the position of an insular power, having less dealings than before with the continent of Europe, but more with the world in general.

13. **America.**—In the **United States** this has been a time of great advance and of great changes.

Many new states have been formed to the West, and the territory of the Union has long reached to the Pacific Ocean. But the only external war which the States have had was the one with Mexico. The great dominion of **Texas** has also been separated from Mexico, and has become part of the United States. But the great event in American history has been the war between the Northern and Southern States which began in 1861. Several causes led to it, the chief being that slavery, which had long died out in the North, still went on in the South. When **Abraham Lincoln** was chosen President in 1860, **South Carolina** seceded. The other Southern States soon followed her, and set up a separate Confederation called the **Confederate States**, under **Jefferson Davis** as President. The war went on till 1865, when the South had to submit. Since then the Union has been put together again, and slavery has been done away with in all parts of it. Meanwhile in 1862, England, France, and Spain, all had a quarrel with Mexico. Matters were soon settled with England and Spain, but France went on, and tried to set up the Austrian **Archduke Maximilian** with the title of Emperor. But he was never acknowledged by the whole country, and in 1867 he was overthrown and shot by the native President **Juares**. Thus Brazil still remains the only monarchy in the new world.

14. **Summary.**—Thus in the last sixty years, and especially in the last twenty years, the world has been greatly changed. In Europe France has again, for the third time, tried to get the chief power, but she has been beaten back more thoroughly than at any time before. Germany and Italy have been joined together into great nations, though the union of Germany is less close than the union of Italy. Austria has withdrawn from Germany and Italy to be joined under one sovereign with the independent kingdom of Hungary. In Sweden and Norway the same union of two

kingdoms under one king has gone on and prospered, while in Russia and Poland it soon broke down, and Poland, as a separate state, has been quite wiped out. Denmark has been cut short by the loss of the Duchies; and the Netherlands have been cut into two separate kingdoms. The Ottoman Empire has lost at all points. Greece has become quite independent, and Servia, the Danubian Principalities, and Egypt nearly so. Notwithstanding the check of the Crimean war, the power of Russia remains great in Europe, and it has greatly increased in Asia. In other parts of the world this time has been marked by the wonderful advance of the English-speaking people everywhere, both in the British colonies and in the United States. On the whole, the world has greatly gained since the great changes at the end of the last century. Nearly every country is far better off than it was. But the tendency of these later times has been to group Europe together under a few great powers, to lessen the importance of the smaller states, and even wholly to wipe out cities and kingdoms which did great things in past times. But, however we may regret this evil, it is not to be set against the general advance in freedom and good government, as well as in all manner of useful inventions, which marks the times in which we live.

THE END.

www.ingramcontent.com/pod-product-compliance
Lightning Source LLC
Chambersburg PA
CBHW030344170426
43202CB00010B/1241